Essay Index

Essays in

MODERN THOUGHT

∾ *Essays in* ∾
MODERN THOUGHT

COLLECTED BY
THOMAS R. COOK

Essay Index Reprint Series

BOOKS FOR LIBRARIES PRESS, INC.
FREEPORT, NEW YORK

First Published 1935
Reprinted 1968

LIBRARY OF CONGRESS CATALOG CARD NUMBER:

68-16922

CONTENTS

iii

INTRODUCTION

One is apt to think instinctively, in connection with essay-reading, of a wordy treatise, formal and probably dry, headed by the austere signature of a Francis Bacon. But let us not be frightened away by a word on a book cover, for all of us read essays as chosen fare in the newspapers and current magazines—only they are not headed by the dread term, *Essay*. We never associate the published personalities of some of our popular columnists with the mild, pleasant gossiping of old Samuel Pepys. Yet there is something in common—both give expression to their thoughts on the life around them, with a self-revelation which is the true test of the essayist. We think of Pepys as old, yet it was as a young man that he kept his diary. His stilted mannerisms seem old in light of the pace in writing which we enjoy. So much has journalism changed in recent years, and almost as great, too, has been the change in styles of essay-writing.

We all read essays, whether we know it or not. A glance through the list of authors who have contributed to this volume should reveal many familiar names, some of which you follow with keen enjoyment in the public prints. Most of us pause long enough, before starting for a motion picture theatre, to read some critic's review of the movie being shown. Many of these reviews are in true essay style. We decide gradually upon one critic whose ideas and tastes seem closely to coincide with our own. We look for his comments on pictures showing or to be shown, and are guided by what he says of them. Thus we have picked for ourselves one favorite essayist. In complex political situations we turn often for clear information to one of the outstanding writers on current politics, whose opinions are syndicated and published in newspapers throughout the country. Before making the annual purchase of a book for our aunt's birthday, we turn to the book-review section of our best-liked magazine or newspaper to find what is new and to get the reaction of some critic whose judgment we admire. And in certain moods, when our school work is done, what could be more delightful and relaxing than the absurdities with which Robert Benchley bedecks every ordinary situation? These are just a few examples which show how much we really read essays, hardly realizing that we are doing so.

The essay in all its forms has been discovered to be a bright source of ideas and information on every conceivable subject, and in every conceivable humor. The art of essay-writing, it is generally conceded, began with Michel de Montaigne, son of a wealthy herring merchant of sixteenth-century France. Montaigne's personal reflections on informal topics achieved great popularity in France, and were equally well received when translated into English. His influence is evident in the writings of later English journalists, including, like a parade of the centuries, Francis Bacon, Addison and Steele, Charles Lamb, and Robert Louis Stevenson. Washington Irving was the first American author to achieve fame through his essays, while Ralph Waldo Emerson is called the greatest American essayist.

In the past, schools have been wont to inflict overdoses of formal literature from the pens of writers of an earlier day. This book proposes to leave the beauties of *Sesame and Lilies,* and comparable compositions, for a more mature appreciation, and to concern itself only with modern essays.

Pupils in senior high school are ready to appreciate essays. They have obtained during their earlier school years a grounding in written and oral expression. They should find it profitable and enjoyable to study the technique and styles of various essay-writers. They can appreciate the fluency of smooth structure.

It should be no dull task for senior high-school students to diagnose paragraph building, to consider treatment of theme, methods of creating moods with words. They should find pleasure in analyzing descriptive style. They should go beneath the subject matter, and appraise and appreciate the details of a writer's skill. In brief, they should *learn to read.*

Then they are ready to try their hand at writing. All students are not going to be creative writers, but everyone, whatever his walk in life, needs to be capable of writing a good sentence. Let your first attempts be short, with emphasis placed on sentence structure, unity, coherence, and all the old bugbears of the grammar book. Choose each word as carefully as you choose its place in the sentence, following as a model the form and even the style of some good author. Try for apt phrases and striking effects, avoiding the humdrum and shunning exaggeration. Do not be satisfied with first attempts, but develop a sense of self-criticism. In other words, *learn to write!*

Finally, *learn to speak!* The breach in mental development between civilized man and the savage is said to be as wide as the breach in language. In the case of the average Canadian, the gap is appallingly narrow. A few overworked words, supplemented by gesticulations and meaningless expletives, serve us in expressing all our ideas. Let us be as fastidious in our speech as we are in our personal appearance. Let the impression of good grooming be deepened rather than destroyed when we launch into conversation. Let our vocabularies be adequate, our enunciation distinct, and our voices pleasing to the ear. In short, let our spoken words proclaim a clearness of thought coupled with clearness of enunciation.

Read these essays for the pleasure you get from them, but read them also with the realization that they may offer exemplifications of clear thinking, beautiful language, and interesting ideas on many interesting subjects.

Smiles

A Dog in the House[1]

BURGES JOHNSON

Burges Johnson is a New Englander. He looks like one, talks like one, and has a droll, dry, Yankee kind of humor. He was born in Rutland, Vermont, in 1877, but left early in life, when his father, a clergyman, was assigned to a parish in New London, Connecticut. From New London, the family moved to Chicago, but when ready for college, he returned to New England and entered Amherst, graduating in 1899.

From Amherst, he went to New York, where he found jobs reporting for various metropolitan dailies. Next he became an editorial writer for several magazines, among them *Harper's* and *Putnam's*. He advanced to the position of managing editor of *Outing*, and then editor-in-chief of *Judge*, the humorous weekly. Later, he took a part-time teaching position at Vassar College.

In France during the World War, Mr. Johnson was assigned to recreation duty. "Just stand up," his superior officer advised him, "and tell them some of the old jokes you used to publish when you were editor of *Judge*." "Sir," Johnson says he replied, "when I was editor of *Judge*, we didn't publish any old jokes."

After the War, Dr. Johnson returned to Vassar, and remained there until 1927. Since that time he has been at Syracuse, where he is Professor of English, Director of Public Relations, and advisor on university publications. He is the author of two volumes of essays, *The Well of English and the Bucket* and *As I Was Saying*, several volumes of verse, and has contributed numerous stories, essays, and verses to magazines. Amherst honored him with the degree of Doctor of Letters.

Dr. Johnson is a witty and popular speaker. At the moment he is facing a ponderous question, to which he declares he is seeking an answer. "I spent sixteen years in New York in newspaper and editorial work," he says, "and now I have spent sixteen years in teaching. It is a critical moment for me."

---

[1] Reprinted by special permission of Burges Johnson.

WHEN does a house, slowly emerging from a chaos of lumber, bricks, and mortar, and taking on form and substance, cease to be merely a house and become a home? Surely before it is finished; no house which is the dwelling place of its owners is ever finished. Like the corporeal city of New York, each piece of furniture is on trial, each bit of carpet may be torn up to make way for a successor more in keeping with the owner's present state of prosperity. A woman is the center of the home, to be sure. She is the true home-maker. But it is not Home solely because she is there. Several elements are needed which she welds into one unified whole. Strangely incongruous elements they may be—books; worn furniture, worn in such ways as to prove that it has contributed to comfort, and not merely to appearances; bits of handiwork here and there, embroidery or patches or what you will. Battered toys are a satisfactory element: I do not hold with those household efficiency experts who believe that a child's toy should never be discovered outside of the nursery. Children should be directed to keep their belongings within the nursery, to be sure, but the visitor gains at once a certain feeling of confidence in the homeliness of that home where he stumbles upon a wee fire engine across the doorway or sits upon a crippled doll in the parlor arm-chair.

Pets are an important element. How perfectly a weather-beaten rabbit or a tortoise trailing its broken tether work into the picture! Mr. Noyes has written a poem describing the way in which Nature, with her weather stains, paints the ugly newness out of man-made things. In the same way the director of the home manages somehow to take this broken toy, that old chair, a kitten or two, and all the flotsam and jetsam of living, and piece them together into a more wonderful mosaic than all the arts of our modern civilization have been able to fabricate with other materials.

He seemed all legs, like a cuttle-fish, as I carried him in my arms to the nearest street-car.

"You can't bring a dog like that on here," said the conductor,

"But it's just a young little puppy," I protested.

"Little puppy your grandmother!" said the conductor irrelevantly, and rang his bell.

He would neither walk forward independently, nor be led. Whichever direction I essayed, he braced his feet and slid. I felt that his head, which waggled loosely upon his shoulders, would inevitably pull off, and disclose a long pasteboard neck, after the style of those Easter rabbits that are filled with candy; so I lifted him in my arms again, there in the crowded city streets, intensely conscious of an aroused public amusement as I struggled to re-enfold this or that hairy protruding tentacle.

Experience has taught me that there is no graceful method of carrying either a large puppy or a small boy struggling to be free. City blocks seemed to me that day to be miles in length and the baggage car of my suburban train was a haven of refuge, a flowery bed of ease. Yet always in my mind was the thought that there would be new struggles and humiliations at the final stage of my progress—from train to house. I found myself saying over and over, with all sorts of variations, "Water quench fire, fire burn stick, stick beat dog, for dog and I have *miles* and *miles* to go before we reach home!"

Up a certain new-made path I came, dragging my reluctant quadruped, his legs braced against me, his frowsy neck stretched to the danger point. On the porch, littered with the trash of building operations, stood the home-maker, waving a greeting. Behind her a temporary front door gaped hospitably open. An orchestra of saws and hammers played a rough welcoming chorus. Suddenly the taut chain in my hand grew slack. My sprawly captive wobbled past me, mounted the steps and sat down before the door, facing the path by which we had come. An unknown workman approached with a board upon his shoulder. Our drafted recruit arose to his full stilted height and barked his first warning of danger—barked with such tremulously eager violence that the effort tumbled him over; but behold, he had become a watch-pup, and this was Home!

In time the house stopped growing, at least in outward dimensions. Not so its guardian. He took on length and breadth, and visible cubits were added to his stature with every passing week. As he grew bigger he grew blacker, turning from a dusty nondescript rustiness to a glossy blackness from nose-tip to tail. The Hound of the Baskervilles was with us in the flesh, but not in the spirit. What his spirit was I find it hard to say. Put the soul of Puck into a clumsy container, modify it by an emotionally affectionate temperament, and you have something approximating the truth.

I have never been wholly patient with those who generalize disparagingly about certain breeds of dog. "Fox-terriers," says a certain flat-dweller, "are irritable and snappy." "Collies," says another, "are dangerously temperamental."

Grant me a lively, impetuous disposition and then shut me in a superheated flat many hours of every day, and I will snap. Let me dress you in furs in warm weather and then urge you repeatedly to run and fetch a stick within a narrow yard—you will become dangerously temperamental. Some breeds of dog have certain natural environments. Out of those environments they are uncertain of themselves, often suspicious, and easily startled into regrettable action. Give a collie meadows to roam, sheep to herd, or, lacking sheep, a "gang" of wide-ranging small boys, and his own times for resting, and then you will have one of God's finest gifts to man, a trustworthy responsible dog. Give a fox-terrier earth for digging, small game or fellow pups for fighting, something to chew, something to chase, and he will be as faithful and alert a friend and servant as heart could wish.

Alas for the unhappy lot of many dogs! It is only the exceptional individual in any breed, more often among the bulls and terriers, that finds its natural environment in a city house and street; unless it be for those wee anomalies which Brother Irvin Cobb shockingly alludes to as "fur-bearing cockroaches"; and perhaps also for their first cousins who lack the fur and are ever shivering in consequence. But are they indeed dogs?

As for the dane, because I love the tribe so well I shall speak with diffidence, hesitating at generalizations and holding close to one unmelancholy specimen, which, from puppyhood to elephantine adolescence, bumbled daily from bedroom to garden, from kitchen to attic, making the house and our hearts his own. Yet I am going to venture the following general assertions and then humbly await their destruction at the pen of some wiser caninologist. The dane is no more nearly related to a mastiff than he is to a St. Bernard. The greyhound is his nearest kin. Yet his blundering masters in past years, chiefly in this country, have bred him with thick legs and neck and heavy jowl. Having the heart of a greyhound in the body of a mastiff, he has been as uneasy of spirit as a collie in a city dwelling.

"It is faithful and trustworthy," says a certain encyclopædia, "and when first introduced into England was a favorite companion of both ladies and gentlemen; but when the order came into 'force commanding all dogs to be muzzled, this hound, having a will of its own, rebelled against being held in check, and being very strong, could not easily be kept under control, so had to be abandoned as a companion. It is now chiefly used as a show dog, but in the middle ages it was a sporting dog, and was employed to hunt the wild boar and chase the deer"—and so on, through many highly creditable paragraphs.

Let me hazard another generalization (observe how easily the didactic manner lays hold on one!). A dog possessing speed and strength relies naturally upon those traits in emergency. The instinct of a hunting dane is to hurl its weight upon the foe. Teeth as weapons are an afterthought. A great dane that readily snaps or bites is a dog with misdirected energies.

As for our guardian, he steadily grew in size and glossy blackness, in whimsical mischief, in *personality*, and in devotion. The feeding was no serious matter. He ate everything. Two elements were to be considered in preparing the food—filling and nutrition; two parts filling to one part nutrition. Table scraps of every sort, even to fruit peelings, were grist for his mill. He was not an embarrassment in this regard—he was a useful institution.

An embarrassment he was in many ways. Demonstrations of affection from one hundred and twenty pounds of dog may be

accepted in spirit, but in the flesh they were as the advances of
an amiable earthquake. There would come a troubled look in his
soulful brown eyes when his struggles for some inadequate resting
place upon his mistress's lap went unrewarded; and he would in-
sinuate himself into incredibly small spaces to find room upon a
sofa beside any one of us.

Rebuffs touched him so deeply that they, too, were the cause of
embarrassment. It was his immediate wish when rebuked to retire under something—the lower it was, the better. When his
spirits returned, as they invariably did, and he arose to full height,
forgetting first to crawl out, he was likely to leave the room with a
small table or chair perched jauntily upon his back. Nosing under
a rug was, on the other hand, a constant delight, and I picture
him standing gravely before me with some gaudy Turkish garment that he himself had donned covering him from head to tail,
his bright eyes gleaming up at me from under one end of it while
the other end wagged heavily.

He had the ways of a terrier, and like a handsome boy who has
grown over-tall, he seemed ever to be deploring his size. Perhaps
the safest generalization about a proper dane is to say that either
he never realizes he is not a lapdog, or always regrets that he is not.

Some time ago an old friend whom I had not seen for several
years accosted me in the street.

"Married?" he inquired, after other time-bridging questions.

"Yes."

"Any children?"

"Three. And you?" I added.

"Boy and girl—four and six." Then he looked at me thought-
fully for a moment, seized my lapel and drew me outside the
current of traffic. "You tell me *one* story about your kids," he burst
out, "and I'll tell you one about mine!"

Dog owners are like parents in this respect—on their tongue-
tips hang accounts of precocious acts, or deeds displaying almost
human intelligence, and the careless acquaintance may unwit-
tingly touch some hair-trigger that discharges the whole narration
upon him.

Are you not, gentle dog-owning reader, pursuing these very pages with a certain friendly impatience, your thoughts flitting back and forth from your dog to mine? Are you not quivering to interrupt at my first pause for breath, with a "How interesting!— But I must tell you about our Fido—you've no idea how bright he is."

I will gladly listen to your panegyric, when you have heard mine.

I will even love your dog with you—if he be a *real* dog—on your say-so. Ah me, how easy it is to come to love a dog! And when there is so much dog to love, his hold upon one's affection becomes very great. "No man is so poor," says Josh Billings, "but what he can own a dog, and I have known some so poor they owned three." I am poor enough to have owned several sizes of dog; but without disparagement of any lesser breed within the law I exhort you at one time or another in your lives, for your soul's good, to get to know a dane. I would have you watch this giant body with its heart of a child gravely stalking some small beetle through the grass. I would have you note his lofty condescension toward in-imical small dogs—his eager playfulness with friendly ones who always enter into games with him in a spirit of fearful bravado, wagging their tails violently throughout, as an earnest that no chance act of theirs should be misunderstood.

I would have you see him dig—not merely to hide a bone, but for the fun of digging. A wonder to the neighborhood was the hole our black genie dug beneath an ancient tree-stump. Straight into the ground he would crawl—under and between the roots com-pletely out of sight; emerging finally on the other side like some buried mammoth exhuming itself.

I would have you swim with him, for his speed and power and reserve strength in the water are joys to behold. Often have I, and others with me, held to a powerful black tail and trailing out al-most flat on the water been drawn many yards to shore.

Though a dane be first cousin to a greyhound, his tail is surely younger brother to that of a kangaroo. It steers him, it balances him like a gyroscope, and when he would bring his great weight to a sudden stop, it goes round and round in swift revolutions like a reversed propeller on an airship. He is forever flailing it against some unfriendly corner and bruising the tip; then—yes, I admit it to his disadvantage—he goes about slapping little blood marks against walls and whimpering in grieved surprise at each new pain.

Obviously there are disadvantages to a dane. Humbug though he be ofttimes, since he has the dignity and bearing of a panther timid strangers refuse to consider him a humbug. Well-intentioned though he is, yet those growls that seem to emanate from some sub-basement of his physical structure are enough indication for many sceptic friends, who prefer not to trust to his intentions. He is not a wise investment for gregarious folk in a crowded neighborhood. And yet in my effort toward a dispassionate consideration I have gone too far. There are many facts on the other side of the scale. He will not fight with neighbors' dogs—he is too big. Little aggressors he bowls over with a blow of his shoulder. As a draft animal for the children who come to know him he is invaluable, and for the littlest he is better than a dozen hobby horses.

Yes, thou unbeliever, I grant that this is a picture of one particular dane, drawn from loving memory. I will believe your stories of this or that dangerous monster of a beast. But I have heard, too, of treacherous collies and even mad poodles; and on the other hand I have learned that there are many other danes like mine; I have learned of them on those pleasant idle occasions when I have happened upon one dane-owner or another, and stepping out of the stream of traffic for a moment have listened to one story about his dog and told him one about mine.

Humbug was a term I used a moment ago, and though it may be written with a smile, yet there are good grounds for it now and then. Since knowing and coming to love the breed I have entered a kennel of strange danes, whose basso profundo growls and gnashing teeth seemed to welcome me to instant destruction. I have not, I assure you, the disposition of a lion tamer. It was simply that each stately head and lithe body seemed to be but a replica of my own dog-chum, clad for the moment perhaps in some other colored garment. And as I pushed through the gate I found myself swayed this way and that by struggling monsters who wished to have their heads scratched. Listen to this corroborative testimony from a friend. She visited her Adirondack camp after a long absence. Dane pups had been born and had grown to dog's estate since she had last inspected the property. She missed her guide and caretaker at the station, and went alone to the camp, where no one was on hand to greet her. Letting herself in at the front door she was startled by a chorus of blood-curdling growls, and found herself facing three full-grown danes on guard.

"I had heard it said," she told us in recounting the affair, "that one's only safety when at the mercy of fierce animals lies in calm and ordinary behavior. With my heart beating violently, I looked for some commonplace act to perform. Ashes had blown out from the fireplace over the floor. A broom stood handily by. The moment I reached for it those formidable beasts leaped, as one dog, out of the room. One of them went through an unopened window, taking the sash with him. It seems that the broom handle which I had touched was the utensil used by my guide for maintaining discipline among the dogs."

We miss our black familiar—miss his inquiring whine at the door of a morning, his companionship upon every sort of expedition, his petty sins and his contrition, his humbuggery, his enormous weeping for infinitesimal punishments. We miss him as a warm footstool beneath the table where he would lie patiently throughout meal time, happy to serve in that humble capacity. And if this be his individual picture, painted with the colors of prejudice, as a sort of memorial to a dead friend, yet I dare assert that here and there among my readers dane-owners will cry out, "He might have meant our Bismarck, our Prince, our Osra, when he wrote that!"

The Happiest Half-Hours of Life [1]

A. A. MILNE

A. A. Milne has won his greatest fame as the father of Christopher Robin and the author of the charming adventures of that child and his companions, Pooh, Piglet, and the others. The charm and originality of Milne's children's stories have earned him a place among the few authors who produce real literature for children. By the lightness which characterizes Milne's writing —whether essay, play, novel, or Winnie-the-Pooh adventure—he has acquired the indelible stamp of whimsicality. He accepts the classification somewhat ruefully. In the preface to his play, *The Ivory Door*, Mr. Milne soliloquizes: "It is always a convenience to have a writer labeled and card-indexed. I have the whimsical label so firmly round my own neck that I can neither escape from it nor focus it."

Alan Alexander Milne was born in London in 1882. He attended school at Westminster and Trinity College, Cambridge, where he edited the college literary paper, the *Granta*. He started at once on a journalistic career, and soon became assistant editor of the humorous magazine, *Punch*, which post he held for eight years.

In the War, Mr. Milne served with the Royal Warwickshire Regiment. At a training camp for officers he found time to write his first play, *Wurzel-Flummery*, a satirical comedy. Later, while he was assigned to duty as an instructor in signaling, he worked nights to complete three more plays.

His old position on *Punch* was open to him after demobilization, but he chose to devote all his time to creative writing. He brought out three books of essays, and more plays. Then, about 1923, his own small son provided the inspiration for the Christopher Robin verses and stories, *When We Were Very Young*, *Now We Are Six*, and the rest, which have delighted so many other children, and their elders as well.

[1] Taken from *Not That It Matters*, by A. A. Milne, published and copyrighted by E. P. Dutton and Company, New York.

YESTERDAY I should have gone back to school, had I been a hundred years younger.

My most frequent dream nowadays—or nowanights I suppose I should say—is that I am back at school, and trying to construe difficult passages from Greek authors unknown to me. That they are unknown is my own fault, as will be pointed out to me sternly in a moment. Meanwhile I stand up and gaze blankly at the text, wondering how it is that I can have forgotten to prepare it. "Er —him the—er—him the—the er many-wiled Odysseus—h'r'm— then, him addressing, the many-wiled Odysseus—er—addressed. Er—er—the er——" And then, sweet relief, I wake up. That is one of my dreams; and another is that I am trying to collect my books for the next school and that an algebra, or whatever you like, is missing. The bell has rung, as it seems hours ago, I am searching my shelves desperately, I am diving under my table, behind the chair . . . I shall be late, I shall be late, late, late. . . .

No doubt I had these bad moments in real life a hundred years ago. Indeed I must have had them pretty often that they should come back to me so regularly now. But it is curious that I should never dream that I am going back to school, for the misery of going back must have left a deeper mark on my mind than all the little accidental troubles of life when there. I was very happy at school; but oh, the utter wretchedness of the last day of the holidays!

One began to be apprehensive on the Monday. Foolish visitors would say sometimes on the Monday, "When are you going back to school?" and make one long to kick them for their tactlessness. As well might they have said to a condemned criminal, "When are you going to be hanged?" or, "What kind of—er—knot do you think they'll use?" Throughout Monday and Tuesday we played the usual games, amused ourselves in the usual way, but with heavy hearts. In the excitement of the moment we would forget and be happy, and then suddenly would come the thought, "We're going back on Wednesday."

And on Tuesday evening we would bring a moment's comfort to ourselves by imagining that we were not going back on the morrow. Our favorite dream was that the school was burnt down early on Wednesday morning, and that a telegram arrived at breakfast apologizing for the occurrence, and pointing out that it would be several months before even temporary accommodation could be erected. No Vandal destroyed historic buildings so light-heartedly as we. And on Tuesday night we prayed that, if the lightnings of Heaven failed us, at least a pestilence should be sent in aid. Somehow, *somehow*, let the school be uninhabitable!

But the telegram never came. We woke on Wednesday morning as wakes the murderer on his last day. We took a dog or two for a walk; we pretended to play a game of croquet. After lunch we donned the badges of our servitude. The comfortable, careless, dirty flannels were taken off, and the black coats and stiff white collars put on. At 3:30 an early tea was ready for us—something rather special, a last mockery of holiday. (Dressed crab, I remember, on one occasion, and I traveled with my back to the engine after it—a position I have never dared to assume since.) Then good-byes, tips, kisses, a last look, and—the 4:10 was puffing out of the station. And nothing, nothing had happened.

I can remember thinking in the train how unfair it all was. Fifty-two weeks in the year, I said to myself, and only fifteen of them spent at home. A child snatched from his mother at nine, and never again given back to her for more than two months at a time. "Is this Russia?" I said; and, getting no answer, could only comfort myself with the thought, "This day twelve weeks!"

And once the incredible did happen. It was through no intervention of Providence; no, it was entirely our own doing. We got near some measles, and for a fortnight we were kept in quarantine. I can say truthfully that we never spent a duller two weeks. There seemed to be nothing to do at all. The idea that we were working had to be fostered by our remaining shut up in one room most of the day, and within the limits of that room we found very little in the way of amusement. We were bored extremely. And always we carried with us the thought of Smith or Robinson taking our place in the Junior House team and making hundreds of runs. . . .

Because, of course, we were very happy at school really. The trouble was that we were so much happier in the holidays. I have had many glorious moments since I left school, but I have no doubt as to what have been the happiest half-hours in my life. They were the half-hours on the last day of term before we started home. We spent them on a lunch of our own ordering. It was the first decent meal we had had for weeks, and when it was over there were all the holidays before us. Life may have better half-hours than that to offer, but I have not met them.

The Tortures of Week-End Visiting [1]

ROBERT C. BENCHLEY

Robert Charles Benchley, the genial dramatic critic of the *New Yorker*—if a dramatic critic is ever called genial—has been at the business of writing ever since his college days. A member of the Harvard Class of 1912, he wrote for the college newspaper, and illustrated his writings with caricatures. Benchley was the most popular boy in Harvard, and a member of every club there. He became engaged in his freshman year to the girl who later became his wife.

Robert Benchley was born in Worcester, Massachusetts, in 1889. Left an orphan in his infancy, he was adopted by a family who gave him many opportunities to develop his talents. He went from Harvard directly to the advertising department of the *Saturday Evening Post*, to begin a career which was to bring him fame as author, dramatic critic, and actor in movie "shorts." He contributes regularly to *Life* and the *New Yorker*, and wrote, among his many other delightful articles, a particularly appropriate introduction to one of those question books with which witty American hostesses used to make a guest's evening intolerable.

Robert Benchley lives in New York and travels much in Europe.

ᔭ ᔭ

THE present labor situation shows to what a pretty pass things may come because of a lack of understanding between the parties involved. I bring in the present labor situation just to give a touch of timeliness to this thing. Had I been writing for the Christmas number, I should have begun as follows: "The indiscriminate giving of Christmas presents shows to what a pretty pass things may come because of a lack of understanding between the parties involved."

The idea to be driven home is that things may come to a pretty

[1] From *Of All Things*, by Robert Benchley. Copyright, Henry Holt and Company. By permission of the publishers.

pass by the parties involved in an affair of any kind if they do not come to an understanding before commencing operations.

I hope I have made my point clear. Especially is this true (watch out carefully now, as the whole nub of the article will be coming along in just a minute), especially is this true in the relations between host and guest on week-end visits. (There, you have it! In fact, the title to this whole thing might very well be, "The Need for a Clearer Definition of Relations between Host and Guest on Week-end Visits," and not be at all overstating it, at that.)

The logic of this will be apparent to any one who has ever been a host or a guest at a week-end party, a classification embracing practically all Caucasians over eleven years of age who can put powder on the nose or tie a bow-tie. Who has not wished that his host would come out frankly at the beginning of the visit and state, in no uncertain terms, the rules and preferences of the household in such matters as the breakfast hour? And who has not sounded his guest to find out what he likes in the regulation of his diet and *modus vivendi* (mode of living)? Collective bargaining on the part of labor unions and capital makes it possible for employers to know just what the workers think on matters of common interest. Is collective bargaining between host and guest so impossible, then?

Take, for example, the matter of arising in the morning. Of course, where there is a large house-party the problem is a simple one, for you can always hear the others pattering about and brushing their teeth. You can regulate your own arising by the number of people who seem to be astir. But if you are the only guest there is apt to be a frightful misunderstanding.

"At what time is breakfast?" you ask.

"Oh, any old time on Sundays," replies the hostess with a generous gesture. "Sleep as late as you like. This is 'Liberty Hall.' "

The sentiment in this attitude is perfectly bully, but there is nothing that you can really take hold of in it. It satisfies at the time, but in the morning there is a vagueness about it that is simply terrifying.

Let us say that you awake at eight. You listen and hear no one stirring. Then, over on the cool pillow again until eight-twenty. Again up on the elbow, with head cocked on one side. There is a creak in the direction of the stairs. They may all be up and going down to breakfast! It is but the work of a moment, to bound out of bed and listen at the door. Perhaps open it modestly and peer out. Deathlike silence, broken only, as the phrase goes, by the ticking of the hall clock, and not a soul in sight. Probably they are late sleepers. Maybe eleven o'clock is their Sunday rising hour. Some people *are* like that.

Shut the door and sit on the edge of the bed. More sleep is out of the question. Let's take a look at the pictures in the guest-room, just to pass the time. Here's one of Lorna Doone. How d'e do, Lorna? Here's a group—taken in 1902—showing your host in evening clothes, holding a mandolin. Probably a member of his college musical club. Rather unkempt looking bunch, you *must* say. Well, how about this one? An etching, showing suspicious-looking barges on what is probably the Thames. Fair enough, at that.

Back to the door and listen again. Tick-tock-tick-tock. Probably, if you started your tub, you'd wake the whole house. Let's sit down on the edge of the bed again.

Hello, here are some books on the table. *Fifty Famous Sonnets*, illustrated by Maxfield Parrish. Never touch a sonnet before breakfast. *My Experiences in the Alps*, by a woman mountain-climber who has written on the fly-leaf, "To my good friends the Elbridges, in memory of many happy days together at Chamounix. October, 1907." That settles *that*. *Essay on Compensation* in limp leather, by R. W. Emerson, published by Houghton, Mifflin & Co. Oh, very well! You suppose they thought that would be over your head, did they? Well, we'll just show them! We'll read it just for spite. Opening, to the red ribbon:

"Of the like nature is that expectation of change which instantly follows the suspension of our voluntary activity. The terror of cloudless noon—"

By the way, it must be nearly noon now! Ten minutes past nine, only! Well, the only thing to do is get dressed and go out and walk about the grounds. Eliminate the tub as too noisy. And so, very cautiously, almost clandestinely, you proceed to dress.

And now, just to reverse the process. Suppose you are the host. You have arisen at eight and listened at the guest's door. No sound. Tip-toe back and get dressed, talking in whispers to your wife (the hostess) and cramming flannel bears into the infant's mouth to keep him from disturbing the sleeper.

"Bill looked tired last night. Better let him sleep a little longer," you suggest. And so, downstairs on your hands and knees, and look over the Sunday papers. Then a bracing walk on the porch, resulting in a terrific appetite.

A glance at the watch shows nine o'clock. Sunday breakfast is usually at eight-thirty. The warm aroma of coffee creeps in from the kitchen and, somewhere, *some one* is baking muffins. This is awful! You suppose it feels something like this to be caught on an ice-floe without any food and so starve to death. Only there you can't smell coffee and muffins. You sneak into the dining-room and steal one of the property oranges from the sideboard, but little Edgar sees you and sets up such a howl that you have to give it to him. The hostess suggests that your friend may have the sleeping-sickness. Weakened by hunger, you hotly resent this, and one word leads to another.

"Oh, very well, I'll go up and rout him out," you snarl.

Upstairs again, and poise, in listening attitude, just in front of the guest's door. Slowly the door opens, inch by inch, and finally his head is edged cautiously out toward yours.

"Hello, Bill," you say flatly, "what are you getting up this time of the morning for? Thought I told you to sleep late."

"Morning, Ed," he says, equally flatly, "hope I haven't kept you all waiting." Then you both lie and eat breakfast.

Such a misunderstanding is apt to go to almost any length. I once knew of a man on a week-end visit who spent an entire Sunday in his room, listening at his door to see if the family were astir, while, in the meantime, the family, one by one, tiptoed to his door to see if they could detect any signs of life from him.

Each thought the other needed rest.

Along about three in the afternoon the family threw all hospitality aside and ate breakfast, deadening the sound of the cutlery as much as possible, little dreaming that their guest was looking through the "A Prayer for Each Day" calendar for the ninth time and seriously considering letting himself down from the window on a sheet and making for the next train. Shortly after dark persistent rumors got abroad that he had done away with himself, and every one went up and sniffed for gas. It was only when the maid, who was not in on the secret, bolted into the room to turn down his bed for the night, that she found him tip-toeing about, packing and unpacking his bag and listening eagerly at the wall. (Now don't ask how it happened that the maid didn't know that his bed hadn't been made that morning. What difference does it make, anyway? It is such questions as *that*, that blight any attempt at individual writing in this country.)

Don't think, just because I have taken all this space to deal with the rising-hour problem, that there are no other points to be made. Oh, not at all. There is, for instance, the question of exercise. After dinner the host says to himself: "Something must be done. I wonder if he likes to walk." Aloud, he says: "Well, Bill, how about a little hike in the country?"

A hike in the country being the last thing in the world that Bill wants, he says, "Right-o! Anything you say." And so, although walking is a tremendous trial to the host, who has weak ankles, he bundles up with a great show of heartiness and grabs his stick as if this were the one thing he lived for.

After about a mile of hobbling along the country road the host says, hopefully: "Don't let me tire you out, old man. Any time you want to turn back, just say the word."

The guest, thinking longingly of the fireside, scoffs at the idea of turning back, insisting that if there is one thing in all the world that he likes better than walking it is running. So on they jog, hippity-hop, hippity-hop, each wishing that it would rain so that they could turn about and go home.

Here again the thing may go to almost tragic lengths. Suppose neither has the courage to suggest the return move. They might walk on into Canada, or they might become exhausted and have to be taken into a roadhouse and eat a "$2 old-fashioned Southern dinner of fried chicken and waffles." The imagination revolts at a further contemplation of the possibilities of this lack of coöperation between guest and host.

I once visited a man who had an outdoor swimming-pool on his estate. (Consider that as very casually said.) It was in April, long before Spring had really understood what was expected of her. My first night there my host said:

"Are you a morning plunger?"

Thinking that he referred to a tub plunge in a warm bathroom, I glowed and said: "You bet."

"I'll call for you at seven in the morning, then," he said, "and we'll go out to the pool."

It was evidently his morning custom and I wasn't going to have it said of me that a middle-aged man could outdo me in virility. So, at seven in the morning, in a dense fog (with now and then a slash of cold rain), we picked our way out to the pool and staged a vivid Siberian moving picture scene, showing naked peasants bathing in the Nevsky. My visit lasted five days, and I afterward learned, from one to whom my host had confided, that it was the worst five days he had ever gone through, and that he has chronic joint trouble as a result of those plunges. "But I couldn't be outdone by a mere stripling," he said, "and the boy certainly enjoyed it."

All of this might have been avoided by the posting of a sign in a conspicuous place in my bedroom, reading as follows: "Personally, I dislike swimming in the pool at this time of the year. Guests wishing to do so may obtain towels at the desk."

The sign system is the only solution I can offer. It is crude and brutal, but it admits of no misunderstanding. A sign in each guest-room, giving the hours of meals, political and religious preferences of the family, general views on exercise, etc., etc., with a blank for the guest to fill out, stating his own views on these subjects, would make it possible to visit (or entertain) with a sense of security thus far unknown upon our planet.

Real People [1]

SIMEON STRUNSKY

Simeon Strunsky came to this country from Vitebsk, Russia, where he was born in 1879. He attended the public schools of New York City, graduated from Horace Mann High School, and in 1900 from Columbia University.

For six years after his graduation from Columbia Mr. Strunsky served as a department editor for the *New International Encyclopedia*. Since that time he has been in newspaper work, first with the New York *Evening Post*, and next with the New York *Times*, for which he contributes as a weekly feature an essay for the *Times Book Review*. These articles, sometimes serious, sometimes humorous, have a large weekly following.

Among Mr. Strunsky's books and collections of essays are his latest book, *The Rediscovery of Jones*, *Sinbad and His Friends*, *Little Journeys to Paris*, *Belshazzar Court*, his best known, and *Post-Impressions*, from which the following essay was taken.

AMONG the most remarkable people I have never met is the family that has just moved out of the apartment we were going to rent. My knowledge of those strangers is based entirely on odd bits of information casually furnished by the renting agent in the course of a single interview. Yet they are more actual and alive to me than many people with whom I have lived in intimate communion for years. Is it our fate ever to meet? I look forward to the event and dread it. I look forward with eagerness to a new sensation, and I fear lest the reality fall short of the vivid image I have built up with the help of the renting agent.

In the matter of picking out an apartment, it is an invariable rule that I shall inspect the place and decide whether I like it. This I do after Emmeline has paid down a month's rent and

---

[1] Used by permission of the publishers, Dodd, Mead and Company, Inc.

selected the wall paper. On questions of such nature, Emmeline is the Balkan States and I am the European Concert. She creates a *status quo* and I ratify. In the present instance, however, I was really given a free hand. Emmeline admitted she was suffering from headache when she told the renting agent that she rather liked the place. Later she recognized that the rooms were altogether too small. What had swayed her judgment was that the bedrooms had the sun in the morning and we should thus be saving on our doctor's bills. In this respect expensive apartments are like high-powered motor cars and a long summer vacation on the St. Lawrence. They may be all easily paid for by cutting in two the doctor's annual bills, amounting to ninety-odd dollars. However, I understood that this time Emmeline would be glad to be overruled.

The European Concert had its first shock when it was confronted with the size of the nursery bedroom. The renting agent called my attention to the wall paper. It had a very pretty border, showing scenes from Mother Goose; this at once revealed the purpose for which the room was intended. But I pointed out to him that if we put a chest of drawers against the wall and a little armchair in the corner, the crib would come hard against the steam pipe and would project halfway across the window.

"Oh," he said, looking up in surprise. "There's a crib?"

"Naturally," I said, "we should want this nursery for the baby."

This did not seem to strike him as altogether unreasonable, but he was puzzled nevertheless.

"You see," he explained, "the people who were here before you had a radio."

When a renting agent discerns signs of disappointment in a prospective tenant he immediately calls his attention to the shower. The agent's face as he ushered me into the bathroom and pointed to the shower was irradiated by a smile of ecstatic beatitude. He reminded me of Madame Nazimova when she waits for the Master Builder to tumble from the church tower.

"Does the shower work?" I asked.

"Why, of course it does," he said.

"That is very interesting," I said. "Most of them either drip or else the hot water comes down all at once. I don't suppose you have to keep away to one side and thrust your finger forward timidly before you venture under the shower?"

"Not at all," he said. "This has splendid pressure. Just turn it on for yourself."

I did as I was told, and after he had finished drying himself with his handkerchief he asked me whether this wasn't one of the best showers I had ever come across. I agreed, and he then told me that the very latest ideas in modern bathroom construction had been utilized by the architect. As for the people who had just moved out, they were so delighted with the shower that they spent the greater part of the day in the tub, often doing their reading there.

On our way toward the library and living-room he called my attention to the air in the hall. He said that if there was any breeze stirring anywhere we were sure to get it in that particular apartment. This puzzled me, because he had told Emmeline the same thing about another apartment which she had inspected and which faces south and west, while this one faces north and east. Suppose now a good northeast breeze—But we were now in the main bedroom, and he was asking me to take notice of a small iron safe let into the wall at the height of one's head.

"This," he said, "is extremely useful for jewels and old silver. You don't find it in every apartment house, I assure you."

"That *is* convenient," I said, and looked out of the window; "and of course one could keep other valuables in there, too, like bonds and mortgages and such things."

"A great many people do," he said.

We passed another bedroom which was so small that even the agent looked apologetic. He said it was the maid's room, but that the people who had just moved out had a woman come in by the day and used the chamber as a store-room. He supposed we should prefer to have our maid sleep in the house.

"We do," I said, "but then we might get a short maid. The

Finns, for example, are a notoriously chunky race and attain their full height at an early age. Let us look at the library."

I did not like the room at all. It faced north and looked out upon the rear of.a tall building only thirty feet away. I asked him if the light was always as bleak as it was today.

"You get all the light you want in here," he said. "Lots of people, you know, object to the sun. It's hard on the eyes. The people who had this apartment always kept the window shades down. It made the room so cosy."

I shook my head. The dimensions of the room were quite disappointing. It was not only small, but there was little wall space, because the architect had provided no less than three doorways which were supposed to be covered with portières. I presume that architects find open doorways much easier to plan than any other part of a room.

He was surprised at my objections. There was plenty of space, he thought. As libraries go, it was one of the largest he had seen. Here you put an armchair, and here you put a small, compact writing-desk, and you had plenty of floor space in the middle for a small table.

"And the bookcases?" I asked.

He looked downcast.

"You have bookcases?" he said.

"We have six."

He was about to say something, but I anticipated him.

"I know, of course," I said, "that the people who lived here before used to keep their books in the kitchen, but I hardly see how we could manage that. It's too much trouble, and besides I am somewhat absent-minded. It would be absurd if I should walk into the kitchen for a copy of *Man and Superman*, and come back with half a grapefruit on a plate. And, furthermore, I like a library where a man can get up occasionally from his writing-table and pace up and down while he is clarifying his ideas. You couldn't do that here."

"There is a nice, long hall," he said. "You might pace up and down that." But he saw I was unconvinced, and he did not go to much pains in exhibiting the dining-room, merely remarking that it did look rather small, but the people who last lived in the apartment were accustomed to go out for their meals.

You will see now why I am so intensely interested in the tenants whose successors we were on the point of being. With life growing more flat and monotonous about us, how refreshing to come across a family which keeps a radio in the nursery, does its reading in the bath tub, and never eats in the dining-room. Is it studied originality on their part, or are they born rebels? And how far does their eccentricity go? Does the head of the house, when setting out for his office in the morning, walk upstairs? Do they walk downstairs when they wish to go to bed?

I am still to meet these highly original citizens of New York, but their numbers must be increasing. Every year I hear of more and more former tenants who prefer dark rooms and libraries without shelf space. I have never asked the renting agent why, being so contented with their surroundings, his tenants should have moved out. But probably it is because they have found an apartment where the rooms are still smaller and the windows have no sun at all.

Wit versus Humor

On the Difference between
Wit and Humor [1]

CHARLES S. BROOKS

Charles Stephen Brooks forsook a successful business to pursue the uncertain career of a writer. After graduation from Yale in 1900 he served as a member of his father's printing business in Cleveland, during which time he wrote nothing more than a few magazine articles. He had written in Yale, "only just enough," he says, "to be put on the board in senior year of one of the lesser monthlies—the *Yale Courant*—and at that it was an honorary title rather than participation."

In 1915, when he was thirty-seven years old, Mr. Brooks retired from business. "For the pleasure of a job I liked," he says, "I sacrificed not less than ten to fifteen thousand dollars a year, but the change of occupation was worth it, and I have never regretted my decision.

"New York was opportunity, and for three years, to overcome my tardy start, I kept my nose closely to my desk—lonely years in part, for I had cut the string that held me to my friends. Men younger than myself were far ahead, and it was my task to trot a little faster through longer hours to gain a yard or so on my handicap, but business instructed me to work upon necessity and not wait for a rising wind of inspiration. I learned that only in long hours, in full and exacting days, may success be won."

It is the aim of this writer to publish one book a year. The writing of this one book, and the study required for it, are enough to keep him at his desk about six hours each day.

To other people who might entertain the idea of becoming writers, Mr. Brooks consents to make these suggestions: "If they want to make money, they must study the market, and be sure to write what the public wants. Most of the successful money-seekers take pains to write down to the level of a common under-

---

[1] From *Chimney-Pot Papers*, by Charles S. Brooks, through arrangement with the Yale University Press, Publishers.

standing. It is needless to say that this method does not produce literature, merely a livelihood. I believe that for honest work in literature, either one must pursue it as an avocation, with a job outside to pay the bills, or he must have an independent income, unless, of course, he is willing to put up with hardships and live under a roof at the top of a series of uncarpeted stairways. Remarkable writers do, of course, make ten-strikes, but these very gifted persons are the exception. The most pathetic case is that of a man who says to himself that he will dash off a few pot-boilers and then live off their profits while he turns to something better. Most of these persons, if they make their pile, continue under the persuasion of editors to turn out cheap and profitable yellow pulp. I have known several writers of this kind, and they were disillusioned and disgusted with themselves. Always in their brains was the thought of a worthy book that was no longer within their possibilities. A year of newspaper writing should teach a novice a certain facility; but if he sticks too long in this hasty sort of writing he will probably lose all appreciation of the subtlety of words, of their cadence, and overtone, of all the mystery that accompanies a page that dips down below the surface to a third dimension."

Among Mr. Brooks's popular collections of essays and travel books are the following titles: *There's Pippins and Cheese to Come, Chimney-Pot Papers, Like Summer's Cloud, Hints to Pilgrims, A Thread of English Road,* and *Roundabout to Canterbury.*

I AM not sure that I can draw an exact line between wit and humor. Perhaps the distinction is so subtle nat only those persons can decide who have long white beards. But even an ignorant man, so long as he is clear of Bedlam, may have an opinion.

I am quite positive that of the two, humor is the more comfortable and more livable quality. Humorous persons, if their gift is genuine and not a mere shine upon the surface, are always agreeable companions and they sit through the evening best. They have pleasant mouths turned up at the corners. To these corners the great Master of marionettes has fixed the strings and he holds them in his nimble fingers to twitch them at the slightest jest. But the mouth of a merely witty man is hard and sour until the moment of its discharge. Nor is the flash from a witty man always comforting, whereas a humorous man radiates a general pleasure and is like another candle in the room.

I admire wit, but I have no real liking for it. It has been too often employed against me, whereas humor is always an ally. It never points an impertinent finger into my defects. Humorous persons do not sit like explosives on a fuse. They are safe and easy comrades. But a wit's tongue is as sharp as a donkey driver's stick. I may gallop the faster for its prodding, yet the touch behind is too persuasive for any comfort.

Wit is a lean creature with sharp, inquiring nose, whereas humor has a kindly eye and comfortable girth. Wit, if it be necessary, uses malice to score a point—like a cat, it is quick to jump—but humor keeps the peace in an easy chair. Wit has a better voice in a solo, but humor comes into the chorus best. Wit is as sharp as a stroke of lightning, whereas humor is diffuse like sunlight. Wit keeps the season's fashions and is precise in the phrases and judgments of the day, but humor is concerned with homely, eternal things. Wit wears silk, but humor in home-spun endures the wind. Wit sets a snare, whereas humor goes off whistling without a victim in its mind. Wit is sharper company at table, but humor serves better in mischance and in the rain. When it tumbles wit is sour, but humor goes uncomplaining without its dinner. Humor laughs at another's jest and holds its sides, while wit sits wrapped in study for a lively answer. But it is a workaday world in which we live, where we get mud upon our boots and come weary to the twilight—it is a world that grieves and suffers from many wounds in these years of war: and therefore as I think of my acquaintance, it is those who are humorous in its best and truest meaning rather than those who are witty who give the more profitable companionship.

And then, also, there is wit that is not wit. As someone has written:

> Nor ever noise for wit on me could pass,
> When through the braying I discerned the ass.

I sat lately at dinner with a notoriously witty person (a really witty man) whom our hostess had introduced to provide the entertainment. I had read many of his reviews of books and plays, and while I confess their wit and brilliancy, I had thought them to be hard and intellectual and lacking in all that broader base of humor which aims at truth. His writing—catching the bad habit of the time—is too ready to proclaim a paradox and to assert the unusual, to throw aside in contempt the valuable hay-stack in a fine search for a paltry needle. His reviews are seldom right—as most of us see the right—but they sparkle and hold one's interest for their perversity and unexpected turns.

In conversation I found him much as I had found him in his writing—although, strictly speaking, it was not a conversation, which requires an interchange of word and idea and is turn about. A conversation should not be a market where one sells and another buys. Rather, it should be a bargaining back and forth, and each person should be both merchant and buyer. My rubber plant for your victrola, each offering what he has and seeking his deficiency. It was my friend B—— who fairly put the case when he said that he liked so much to talk that he was willing to pay for his audience by listening in his turn.

But this was a speech and a lecture. He loosed on us from the cold spigot of his intellect a steady flow of literary allusion—a practice which he professes to hold in scorn—and wit and epi-gram. He seemed torn from the page of Meredith. He talked like ink. I had believed before that only people in books could talk as he did, and then only when their author had blotted and scratched their performance for a seventh time before he sent it to the printer. To me it was an entirely new experience, for my usual acquaintances are good common honest daytime woolen folk and they seldom average better than one bright thing in an evening.

At first I feared that there might be a break in his flow of speech which I should be obliged to fill. Once, when there was a slight pause—a truffle was engaging him—I launched a frail re-mark; but it was swept off at once in the renewed torrent. And seriously it does not seem fair. If one speaker insists—to change the figure—on laying all the cobbles of the conversation, he should at least allow another to carry the tarpot and fill in the chinks. When the evening was over, although I recalled two or three clever stories, which I shall botch in the telling, I came away tired and dissatisfied, my tongue dry with disuse.

Now I would not seek that kind of man as a companion with whom to be becalmed in a sailboat, and I would not wish to go to the country with him, least of all to the North Woods or any place outside of civilization. I am sure that he would sulk if he were deprived of an audience. He would be crotchety at breakfast across his bacon. Certainly for the woods a humorous man is better company, for his humor in mischance comforts both him and you. A humorous man—and here lies the heart of the matter —a humorous man has the high gift of regarding an annoyance in the very stroke of it as another man shall regard it when the annoyance is long past. If a humorous man falls out of a canoe he knows the exquisite jest while his head is still bobbing in the cold water. A witty man, on the contrary, is sour until he is changed and dry: but in a week's time when company is about, he will make a comic story of it.

My friend A—— with whom I went once into the Canadian woods has genuine humor, and no one can be a more satisfactory comrade. I do not recall that he said many comic things, and at bottom he was serious, as the best humorists are. But in him there was a kind of joy and exaltation that lasted throughout the day. If the duffle were piled too high and fell about his ears, if the dinner was burned, or the tent blew down in a driving storm at night, he met these mishaps as though they were the very things he had come north to get, as though without them the trip would have lacked its spice. This is an easy philosophy in retrospect but hard when the wet canvas falls across you and the rain beats in. A—— laughed at the very moment of disaster as another man will laugh later in an easy chair. I see him now swinging his axe for firewood to dry ourselves when we were spilled in a rapids; and again, while pitching our tent on a sandy beach when another storm had drowned us. And there is a certain cry of his (dully, *Wow!* on paper) expressive to the initiated of all things gay, which could never issue from the mouth of a merely witty man.

Real humor is primarily human—or divine, to be exact—and after that the fun may follow naturally in its order. Not long ago I saw Louis Jouvet of the French Company play Sir Andrew Aguecheek. It was a most humorous performance of the part, and the reason is that the actor made no primary effort to be funny. It was the humanity of his playing, making his audience love him first of all, that provoked the comedy. His long thin legs were comical and so was his drawling talk, but the very heart and essence was this love he started in his audience. Poor fellow! how delightfully he smoothed the feathers in his hat! How he feared to fight the duel! It was easy to love such a dear, silly, human fellow. A merely witty player might have drawn as many laughs, but there would not have been the catching at the heart.

As for books and the wit or humor of their pages, it appears that wit fades, whereas humor lasts. Humor uses permanent nut-galls. But is there anything more melancholy than the wit of another generation? In the first place, this wit is intertwined with forgotten circumstance. It hangs on a fashion—on the style of a coat. It arose from a forgotten bit of gossip. In the play of words the sources of the pun are lost. It is like a local jest in a narrow coterie, barren to an outsider. Sydney Smith was the most celebrated wit of his day, but he is dull reading now. *Blackwood's* at its first issue was a witty daring sheet, but for us the pages are stagnant. I suppose that no one now laughs at the witticisms of Thomas Hood. Where are the wits of yesteryear? Yet the humor of Falstaff and Lamb and Fielding remains and is a reminder to us that humor, to be real, must be founded on humanity and on truth.

Humor As I See It [1]

Of the stock jokes relied on by professional humorists, "the one about the college professor," in any of its various guises, always gets a laugh. The college professor for years has been sure-fire as a joke. So when a college professor turns humorist and outshines the wits at their own business, that is an old joke with a new twist.

Doctor Leacock, head of the Department of Economics and Political Science at McGill University, author of a book on political science, and Stephen Butler Leacock, whose *Literary Lapses*, *Nonsense Novels*, and other funny books have set their readers rocking with mirth, are one and the same person.

Of his life, the most interesting account is his own, which appears as a preface to *Sunshine Sketches of a Small Town*. In part it follows:

"I was born at Swanmoor, Hants, England, on December 30, 1869. I am not aware that there was any particular conjunction of the planets at the time, but should think it extremely likely. My parents migrated to Canada in 1876, and I decided to go with them. I was educated at Upper Canada College, Toronto, of which I was head boy in 1887. From there I went to the University of Toronto, where I was graduated in 1891. At the University, I spent my entire time in the acquisition of languages, living, dead and half dead, and knew nothing about the outside world. In this diligent pursuit of words I spent about sixteen hours of each day. Very soon after graduation I had forgotten the languages, and found myself intellectually bankrupt. In other words, I was what is called a distinguished graduate, and as such took to school teaching as the only trade I could find that needed neither experience nor intellect. I spent my time from 1891 to 1899 on the staff of Upper Canada College."

At the University of Chicago, Dr. Leacock received his Ph.D. "The meaning of this degree," he explains, "is that the recipient

[1] From *Laughing with Leacock*, by Stephen Leacock. Used by permission of the author. Copyright by Dodd, Mead and Company, Inc.

of instruction is examined for the last time in his life, and is pronounced completely full. After this no new ideas can be imparted to him."

Referring to his writings, Mr. Leacock says, "The writing of solid, instructive stuff fortified by facts and figures is easy enough. But to write something out of one's own mind, worth reading for its own sake, is an arduous contrivance, only to be achieved in fortunate moments, few and far between. Personally, I should rather have written *Alice in Wonderland* than the whole *Encyclopedia Britannica*."

I T IS only fair that at the back of this book I should be allowed a few pages to myself to put down some things that I really think.

Until two weeks ago I might have taken my pen in hand to write about humor with the confident air of an acknowledged professional.

But that time is past. Such claim as I had has been taken from me. In fact I stand unmasked. An English reviewer writing in a literary journal, the very name of which is enough to put contradiction to sleep, has said of my writing, "What is there, after all, in Professor Leacock's humor but a rather ingenious mixture of hyperbole and myosis?"

The man was right. How he stumbled upon this trade secret, I do not know. But I am willing to admit, since the truth is out, that it has long been my custom in preparing an article of a humorous nature to go down to the cellar and mix up half a gallon of myosis with a pint of hyperbole. If I want to give the article a decidedly literary character, I find it well to put in about half a pint of paresis. The whole thing is amazingly simple.

But I only mention this by way of introduction and to dispel any idea that I am conceited enough to write about humor with the professional authority of Ella Wheeler Wilcox writing about love, or Eva Tanguay talking about dancing.

All that I dare claim is that I have as much sense of humor as other people. And, oddly enough, I notice that everybody else makes this same claim. Any man will admit, if need be, that his sight is not good, or that he cannot swim, or shoots badly with a rifle, but to touch upon his sense of humor is to give him a mortal affront.

"No," said a friend of mine the other day, "I never go to Grand Opera," and then he added with an air of pride—"You see, I have absolutely no ear for music."

"You don't say so!" I exclaimed.

"None!" he went on. "I can't tell one tune from another. I don't know 'Home, Sweet Home' from 'God Save the King.' I can't tell whether a man is tuning a violin or playing a sonata."

He seemed to get prouder and prouder over each item of his own deficiency. He ended by saying that he had a dog at his house that had a far better ear for music than he had. As soon as his wife or any visitor started to play the piano the dog always began to howl—plaintively, he said, as if it were hurt. He himself never did this.

When he had finished I made what I thought a harmless comment.

"I suppose," I said, "that you find your sense of humor deficient in the same way: the two generally go together."

My friend was livid with rage in a moment.

"Sense of humor!" he said. "My sense of humor! Me without a sense of humor! Why, I suppose I've a keener sense of humor than any man, or any two men, in this city!"

From that he turned to bitter personal attack. He said that *my* sense of humor seemed to have withered altogether.

He left me, still quivering with indignation.

Personally, however, I do not mind making the admission, however damaging it may be, that there are certain forms of so-called humor, or, at least, fun, which I am quite unable to appreciate. Chief among these is that ancient thing called the Practical Joke.

"You never knew McGann, did you?" a friend of mine asked me the other day. When I said, "No, I had never known Mc-Gann," he shook his head with a sigh, and said:

"Ah, you should have known McGann. He had the greatest **sense** of humor of any man I ever knew—always **full of jokes. I** remember one night at the boarding house where we were, he stretched a string across the passageway and then rang the dinner bell. One of the boarders broke his leg. We nearly died laughing."

"Dear me!" I said. "What a humorist! Did he often do things like that?"

"Oh, yes, he was at them all the time. He used to put tar in the tomato soup, and beeswax and tin-tacks on the chairs. He was full of ideas. They seemed to come to him without any trouble."

McGann, I understand, is dead. I am not sorry for it. Indeed I think that for most of us the time has gone by when we can see the fun of putting tacks on chairs, or thistles in beds, or live snakes in people's boots.

To me it has always seemed that the very essence of good humor is that it must be without harm and without malice. I admit that there is in all of us a certain vein of the old, original demoniacal humor or joy in the misfortune of another which sticks to us like our original sin. It ought not to be funny to see a man, especially a fat and pompous man, slip suddenly on a banana skin. But it is. When a skater on a pond who is describing graceful circles and showing off before the crowd, breaks through the ice and gets a ducking, everybody shouts with joy. To the original savage, the cream of the joke in such cases was found if the man who slipped broke his neck, or the man who went through the ice never came up again. I can imagine a group of prehistoric men standing round the ice-hole where he had disappeared and laughing till their sides split. If there had been such a thing as a prehistoric newspaper, the affair would have been headed up: "Amusing Incident. Unknown Gentleman Breaks through Ice and Is Drowned."

But our sense of humor under civilization has been weakened. Much of the fun of this sort of thing has been lost on us.

Children, however, still retain a large share of this primitive sense of enjoyment.

I remember once watching two little boys making snowballs at the side of the street and getting ready a little store of them to use. As they worked there came along an old man wearing a silk hat, and belonging by appearance to the class of "jolly old gentle-men." When he saw the boys his gold spectacles gleamed with kindly enjoyment. He began waving his arms and calling, "Now, then, boys, free shot at me! free shot!" In his gayety he had, with-out noticing it, edged himself over the sidewalk on to the street. An express cart collided with him and knocked him over on his back in a heap of snow. He lay there gasping and trying to get the snow off his face and spectacles. The boys gathered up their snow-balls and took a run toward him. "Free shot!" they yelled. "Soak him! Soak him!"

I repeat, however, that for me, as I suppose for most of us, it is a prime condition of humor that it must be without harm or malice, nor should it convey even incidentally any real picture of sorrow or suffering or death. There is a great deal in the humor of Scotland (I admit its general merit) which seems to me, not being a Scotchman, to sin in this respect. Take this familiar story (I quote it as something already known and not for the sake of telling it).

A Scotchman had a sister-in-law—his wife's sister—with whom he could never agree. He always objected to going anywhere with her, and in spite of his wife's entreaties always refused to do so. The wife was taken mortally ill and as she lay dying, she whis-pered, "John, ye'll drive Janet with you to the funeral, will ye no?" The Scotchman, after an internal struggle, answered, "Margaret, I'll do it for ye, but it'll spoil my day."

Whatever humor there may be in this is lost for me by the actual and vivid picture that it conjures up—the dying wife, the darkened room, and the last whispered request.

No doubt the Scotch see things differently. That wonderful people—whom personally I cannot too much admire—always seem to me to prefer adversity to sunshine, to welcome the pros-pect of a pretty general damnation, and to live with grim cheerful-ness within the very shadow of death. Alone among the nations they have converted the devil—under such names as Old Horny —into a familiar acquaintance not without a certain grim charm of his own. No doubt also there enters into their humor something of the original barbaric attitude toward things. For a primitive people who saw death often and at first hand, and for whom the future world was a vivid reality, that could be *felt*, as it were, in the midnight forest and heard in the roaring storm—for such people it was no doubt natural to turn the flank of terror by forcing a merry and jovial acquaintance with the unseen world. Such a practice as a wake, and the merry-making about the corpse, carries us back to the twilight of the world, with the poor savage in his bewildered misery pretending that his dead still lived. Our funeral with its black trappings and its elaborate ceremonies is the lineal descendant of a merry-making. Our undertaker is, by evolution, a genial master of ceremonies, keeping things lively at the death-dance. Thus have the ceremonies and the trappings of death been transformed in the course of ages till the forced gayety is gone, and the black hearse and the gloomy mutes betoken the cold dignity of our despair.

But I fear this article is getting serious. I must apologize.

I was about to say, when I wandered from the point, that there is another form of humor which I am also quite unable to appreciate. This is that particular form of story which may be called, *par excellence*, the English Anecdote. It always deals with persons of rank and birth, and, except for the exalted nature of the subject itself, is, as far as I can see, absolutely pointless.

This is the kind of thing that I mean.

"His Grace the Fourth Duke of Marlborough was noted for the open-handed hospitality which reigned at Blenheim, the family seat, during his régime. One day on going in to luncheon it was discovered that there were thirty guests present, whereas the table only held covers for twenty-one. 'Oh, well,' said the Duke, not a whit abashed, 'some of us will have to eat standing up.' Everybody, of course, roared with laughter."

My only wonder is that they didn't kill themselves with it. A mere roar doesn't seem enough to do justice to such a story as this.

The Duke of Wellington has been made the storm-center of three generations of wit of this sort. In fact the typical Duke of Wellington story has been reduced to a thin skeleton such as this:

"A young subaltern once met the Duke of Wellington coming

out of Westminster Abbey. 'Good morning, your Grace,' he said, 'rather a wet morning.' 'Yes,' said the Duke, with a very rigid bow, 'but it was a damn sight wetter, sir, on the morning of Waterloo.' The young subaltern, rightly rebuked, hung his head."

Nor is it only the English who sin in regard to anecdotes.

One can indeed make the sweeping assertion that the telling of stories as a mode of amusing others ought to be kept within strict limits. Few people realize how extremely difficult it is to tell a story so as to reproduce the real fun of it—to "get it over," as the actors say. The mere "facts" of a story seldom make it funny. It needs the right words, with every word in its proper place. Here and there, perhaps once in a hundred times, a story turns up which needs no telling. The humor of it turns so completely on a sudden twist or incongruity in the dénouement of it that no narrator, however clumsy, can altogether fumble it.

Take, for example, this well-known instance—a story which, in one form or other, everybody has heard.

"George Grossmith, the famous comedian, was once badly run down and went to consult a doctor. It happened that the doctor, though, like everybody else, he had often seen Grossmith on the stage, had never seen him without his make-up and did not know him by sight. He examined his patient, looked at his tongue, felt his pulse and tapped his lungs. Then he shook his head. 'There's nothing wrong with you, sir,' he said, 'except that you're run down from overwork and worry. You need rest and amusement. Take a night off and go and see George Grossmith at the Savoy.'

"'Thank you,' said the patient, 'I *am* George Grossmith.'"

Let the reader please observe that I have purposely told this story all wrongly, just as wrongly as could be, and yet there is something left of it. Will the reader kindly look back to the beginning of it and see for himself just how it ought to be narrated and what obvious error has been made. If he has any particle of the artist in his make-up, he will see at once that the story ought to begin:

"One day a very haggard and nervous-looking patient called at the office of a fashionable doctor, etc., etc."

In other words, the chief point of the joke lies in keeping it concealed till the moment when the patient says, "Thank you, I am George Grossmith." But the story is such a good one that it cannot be completely spoiled even when told wrongly. This particular anecdote has been variously told of George Grossmith, Coquelin, Joe Jefferson, John Hare, Cyril Maude, and about sixty others. And I have noticed that there is a certain type of man who, on hearing this story about Grossmith, immediately tells it all back again, putting in the name of somebody else, and goes into new fits of laughter over it, as if the change of name made it brand new.

But few people, I repeat, realize the difficulty of reproducing a humorous or comic effect in its original spirit.

"I saw Harry Lauder last night," said Griggs, a Stock-Exchange friend of mine, as we walked up town together the other day. "He came onto the stage in kilts" (here Griggs started to chuckle) "and he had a slate under his arm" (here Griggs began to laugh quite heartily), "and he said, 'I always like to carry a slate with me' (of course he said it in Scotch, but I can't do the Scotch the way he does it) 'just in case there might be any figures I'd be wanting to put down'" (by this time Griggs was almost suffocated with laughter)—"and he took a little bit of chalk out of his pocket, and he said" (Griggs was now almost hysterical), "'I like to carry a wee bit chalk along because I find the slate is'" (Griggs was now faint with laughter), "'the slate is—is—not much good without the chalk.'"

Griggs had to stop, with his hand to his side, and lean against a lamp post. "I can't, of course, do the Scotch the way Harry Lauder does it," he repeated.

Exactly. He couldn't do the Scotch and he couldn't do the rich mellow voice of Mr. Lauder and the face beaming with merriment, and the spectacles glittering with amusement, and he couldn't do the slate, nor the "wee bit chalk"—in fact he couldn't do any of it. He ought merely to have said, "Harry Lauder," and leaned up against a post and laughed till he had got over it.

Yet in spite of everything, people insist on spoiling conversation by telling stories. I know nothing more dreadful at a dinner table than one of these amateur raconteurs—except, perhaps, two of them. After about three stories have been told, there falls on the dinner table an uncomfortable silence, in which everybody is aware that everybody else is trying hard to think of another story, and is failing to find it. There is no peace in the gathering again till some man of firm and quiet mind turns to his neighbor and says—"But after all there is no doubt that whether we like it or not prohibition is coming." Then everybody in his heart says, Thank Heaven! and the whole tableful are happy and contented again, till one of the story tellers "thinks of another," and breaks loose.

Worst of all perhaps is the modest story teller who is haunted by the idea that one has heard his story before. He attacks you after this fashion:

"I heard a very good story the other day on the steamer going to Bermuda"—then he pauses with a certain doubt in his face—"but perhaps you've heard this?"

"No, no, I've never been to Bermuda. Go ahead."

"Well, this is a story that they tell about a man who went down to Bermuda one winter to get cured of rheumatism—but you've heard this?"

"No, no."

"Well, he had rheumatism pretty bad and he went to Bermuda to get cured of it. And so when he went into the hotel he said to the clerk at the desk—but perhaps you know this."

"No, no, go right ahead."

"Well, he said to the clerk 'I want a room that looks out over the sea'—but perhaps—"

Now the sensible thing to do is to stop the narrator right at this point. Say to him quietly and firmly, "Yes, I have heard that story. I always liked it ever since it came out in *Titbits* in 1878, and I read it every time I see it. Go on and tell it to me and I'll sit back with my eyes closed and enjoy it."

No doubt the story-telling habit owes much to the fact that

ordinary people, quite unconsciously, rate humor very low: I mean, they underestimate the difficulty of "making humor." It would never occur to them that the thing is hard, meritorious, and dignified. Because the result is gay and light, they think the process must be. Few people would realize that it is much harder to write one of Owen Seaman's "funny" poems in *Punch* than to write one of the Archbishop of Canterbury's sermons. Mark Twain's *Huckleberry Finn* is a greater work than Kant's *Critique of Pure Reason*, and Charles Dickens's creation of Mr. Pickwick did more for the elevation of the human race—I say it in all seriousness—than Cardinal Newman's "Lead, Kindly Light, amid the Encircling Gloom." Newman only cried out for light in the gloom of a sad world. Dickens gave it.

But the deep background that lies behind and beyond what we call humor is revealed only to the few who, by instinct or by effort, have given thought to it. The world's humor, in its best and greatest sense, is perhaps the highest product of our civilization. One thinks here not of the mere spasmodic effects of the comic artist or the blackface expert of the vaudeville show, but of the really great humor which, once or twice in a generation at best, illuminates and elevates our literature. It is no longer dependent upon the mere trick and quibble of words, or the odd and meaningless incongruities in things that strike us as "funny." Its basis lies in the deeper contrasts offered by life itself: the strange incongruity between our aspiration and our achievement, the eager and fretful anxieties of today that fade into nothingness tomorrow, the burning pain and the sharp sorrow that are softened in the gentle retrospect of time, till as we look back upon the course that has been traversed we pass in view the panorama of our lives, as people in old age may recall, with mingled tears and smiles, the angry quarrels of their childhood. And here, in its larger aspect, humor is blended with pathos till the two are one, and represent, as they have in every age, the mingled heritage of tears and laughter that is our lot on earth.

The College Question

Who Should Go to College? [1]

MAX McCONN

Every high-school senior has given consideration to the question
of college. He looks at it from the point of view of whether his
parents can afford to send him; he considers its social advantages
and opportunities for pleasure; he thinks that such a background
will benefit him in whatever career he embarks upon. In the
following article, the subject is treated from another angle—one
which the student too often fails to consider at all. Dr. Max
McConn attempts to tell every boy and girl whether he or she is
likely to succeed in college.

Dr. McConn has been Dean of Lehigh University since 1923.
In that period he has known intimately the problems, struggles,
and qualifications of boys trying to get along in college. A Dean
is elected to his office because of his understanding of the students'
point of view, and because of his wisdom and tact in dealing with
students' difficulties. What Dr. McConn has to say on the subject
"Who Should Go to College?" is therefore of interest to everyone.

Dr. McConn was born in Ironton, Ohio, in 1881. He has been
an educator since his own undergraduate days. He received a
B.A. from the University of Minnesota in 1903, and an M.A. from
the same institution in 1904. He immediately secured a position as
instructor of English at the University of Illinois Academy, and
two years later he was elected principal of that school. In 1910 he
became Registrar at the University of Illinois; in 1920 he was
made assistant to the President of that University; in 1923 he was
elected Dean of Lehigh University, which position he still fills.

He has written several books on educational subjects, and has
contributed articles to such publications as the *Forum*, the *Nation*,
the *Parents' Magazine*, the New York *Times Magazine*, and many
educational journals.

[1] From *Our Children*, edited by Dorothy Canfield Fisher and Sidonie M.
Gruenberg, copyright 1932, published by the Viking Press. Reprinted by permission of Max McConn and the Viking Press.

AFTER high school or prep school, college. Among well-to-do parents in this country during the first three decades of the present century that sequence came to be accepted as normal and well-nigh inevitable. It was taken for granted that every boy and nearly every girl whose parents could possibly afford to send them should go on to college. But, unfortunately, it has become apparent that there are difficulties with this "new minimum standard for the great mass" and one essential point has become clear; that our colleges, as they *are*, are by no means good places for every boy and girl. They are very fine places for some boys and girls, but for a considerable majority they are very bad places. They offer to one particular type of young man and woman quite worthwhile opportunities for mental and moral development; to all other types they offer virtually nothing, and much worse than nothing, namely, frustration and discouragement.

I shall attempt in this article to specify certain criteria and tests which can apply to any child and by means of which can be determined, with reasonable assurance in most cases, whether that child is or is not what college faculties call "college material" —that is, the kind of human material for which the colleges are at present willing and able to provide.

I shall begin with three major criteria. The boy or girl who is to go to college should possess: (1) A fairly high degree of bookish aptitude. (2) An awakened intellectual interest in something. (3) A fairly high degree of self-mastery or capacity for self-direction.

By bookish aptitude I mean merely a capacity or knack for learning quickly and effectively out of books—by the perusal of printed pages. That is only one way of learning; it is not even the best way; the best way is undoubtedly by living and doing. And the second-best way is probably by talking with those who have lived and done.

But the existing college method of learning is almost exclusively bookish. Consequently, the fact that a particular youngster seems alert and keen in practical matters, quick to understand what is said to him and to respond appropriately in word and action, does not necessarily mean that he is "college material." For that he should be also in some fair degree definitely bookish.

It should be noted that bookish aptitude is only one among many valuable kinds of special aptitude or ability. Three of the other kinds are widely recognized; namely, musical ability; "artistic" ability, meaning aptitude for the graphic arts; and histrionic ability. It is quite commonly understood that these are special talents, and that they either may or may not be associated with bookish ability in the same individual. But there are almost certainly other special talents which have not yet been so definitely identified, and which may not be associated with the kind of aptitude needed for book studies in college.

One of these is the special knack which we call "mechanical"— the gift displayed by the boy who without instruction in physics builds complicated radio sets and picks up London or Melbourne, or takes the car to pieces and puts it together again so that it runs better than it did when it came from the factory. Many parents assume that the possession of this mechanical gift means that the boy is an embryo engineer and will infallibly succeed in a college of engineering. Alas, that does not follow. For success even in an engineering college, the most essential aptitude is bookish—in this case an aptitude for mathematics and the exact sciences dependent on mathematics, including physics, chemistry, and mechanics. The mechanical knack is a valuable thing for an engineer to have, and combined with a flair for mathematics it affords a valuable prognosis of success as an engineer. But merely by itself it affords a prognosis only of success as a mechanician—an electrician, a plumber, a garage mechanic, or the like.

There is one other particular aptitude which I want to describe, though I do so with some hesitation because I have never seen it treated by any psychologist as a special talent; but from my own long experience with young people I am almost sure it is practically that. I shall call it, for lack of a better term, personal-relations aptitude—the kind of charm and tact which enable certain attractive youngsters to make friends with everyone, to be instantly *en rapport* with every person they meet, and hence to deal with and manage and lead other people with striking success. This is, of course, one of the most valuable gifts the gods can bestow. It is priceless in personal relationships and in any profession; and in business, under the existing economic system, it is worth more in dollars and cents than the highest intelligence, even genius, of any other kind. But, according to my experience, it has no clear correlation, either positive or negative, with bookish ability. Many who have it are good also at books; but some who have it in high degree are no good at all at books; and, conversely, some who are excellent at books have little or none of this gift. I stress this point because these youngsters always impress other people as highly "intelligent," and it is almost invariably assumed that they are good candidates for college; but scores of young men and women of just this type are "dropped" from colleges every February and June for hopeless ineptitude at bookish tasks.

With this point well hammered home, I turn to the practical question as to how bookish aptitude of the degree necessary for success in college can be identified. How can one determine with respect to a particular boy whether he has this thing or does not have it?

In answer to this question I shall list half a dozen tests which can be applied. But, before naming these tests, I must insert a large CAUTION: *No one of them is dependable by itself.* Each of them is subject to numerous qualifications and sources of error, but a consensus of results of four or five of them is probably trustworthy.

(1) Our first resort will naturally be to the so-called mental tests, which are available nowadays for many children who have come up through fairly progressive school systems. That these successfully measure "general intelligence" (whatever that is), many people doubt, and I am one of the doubters; but I do believe they usually gauge pretty well the much more limited thing we happen to be concerned with here, namely, bookish aptitude. In order to be definite—and warning my readers that I am taking, and am inflicting upon them, the serious risks of definiteness,—I

will say that in my opinion an Intelligence Quotient of 120 on the Binet-Stanford Test, or a comparable rating on other standard tests, is one indication of probable success in college. On the other hand, an IQ of much below 120 at least raises a question as to whether the boy or girl is likely to profit by existing college courses.

(2) Next we may consider the student's rank in his high-school or preparatory school class. To be definite again: a student who ranks in the top third or the top two-fifths of his class in a reasonably good secondary school can probably do college work, but if the student regularly ranks below the second fifth of his class in the high school, there is some real danger that he may not be able to meet even the minimum standard in college.

(3) Is the student at least up with his age-grade?—that is, is he graduating from the senior high school at eighteen? Educational statisticians have repeatedly found a high positive correlation between youthfulness at entrance to college and success in college (as measured by marks). According to these studies a boy or girl who finishes the high school at eighteen is a fair college risk, one who finishes at seventeen is an excellent risk, and one who finishes at sixteen is a very superior risk—will probably win honors. Conversely, the student who does not complete the secondary school course until he is nineteen is a slightly dubious risk, and the one who does not finish until twenty or later is much more doubtful. (In applying this test in an individual case, consideration should, of course, be given to protracted or major interruptions of school life on account of illness, travel, the removal of parents from one city to another, or similar circumstances.)

(4) Reading speed. Rapidity in reading has an obvious direct bearing on success in college work, because of the large amount of reading which must be covered in nearly all college courses. But it is probably also a direct measure of the special kind of aptitude which I am calling bookish, because rapidity of reading usually correlates with comprehension and retention. Generally speaking, the more rapidly a reader reads, the more effectively he grasps and retains. The median reading speed of college freshmen has been

found to be around 250 words a minute on ordinary reading matter, and a student who reads more slowly than that will certainly have difficulty in completing his college tasks within reasonable study periods. To be a really good college risk under this criterion one should readily and habitually cover not fewer than 300 words a minute on ordinary reading matter.

(5) Vocabulary. The possession of a full and accurate vocabulary for recognition and for use is one of the best indications of bookish aptitude. I do not know of any definite form in this matter that can be cited; but I will suggest one rough test that anyone can use; a young man or woman of eighteen who is thoroughly good college material should be able to read aloud a nontechnical article in such a magazine as *Harper's* or the *Atlantic Monthly* with practically no stumbling over the pronunciation or meaning of words.

(6) Does the prospective college student show some predilection for the use of dictionaries, encyclopedias, gazetteers, maps, and the like? In other words, does he or she evince some appetite for precise information, with the habit of going to the recognized sources of such information? I am not prepared to say that the absence of this predilection and habit is significant; but its presence can be scored as an excellent indication of bookish aptitude.

The second and third major criteria suggested at the beginning of this chapter probably need only brief elaboration.

The second one was—it may be remembered—an awakened intellectual interest in something. Under modern conditions all children must become literate and must therefore attend the elementary school. Perhaps all, or as many as possible, should go into the secondary schools, whether they take any interest in book learning or not—though of this I am far from sure. But in any case there seems to be no good reason why any young man or woman should proceed with advanced studies at the college level unless there is at least one subject he or she has enjoyed studying and really wants to go on studying. To me this seems axiomatic.

There is a fair number of young men and women of eighteen or thereabouts who have numerous intellectual interests—who

sincerely want to learn more about many things. From the stand-
point of this criterion these are ideal candidates for college. Then
there is a larger number of young people who display no great
enthusiasm for most subjects of instruction, but are genuinely
keen in some one field of intellectual interests, whether poetry or
anthropology or psychology or banking or international relations
or mathematics or geology or biology or chemistry or electrical
engineering or forestry or interior decoration or counterpoint or
what else. I would say that if there is any subject whatever that is
taught in college which a young man or woman has definitely
enjoyed studying and really wants to go on studying, then that
young person qualifies for college under this heading. But if no
such subject can be discovered, then I should not send that
student to college—at least not yet.

My third major criterion—a fairly high degree of self-mastery—
is not intellectual, like the first two, but moral. Its importance
arises from the fact that the colleges—whether they should do so
or not—throw their students almost wholly upon their own responsibility for their personal living and even for their attention
to studies.

How can one tell in advance whether a particular boy, let us
say, meets this criterion? That is comparatively easy. One has
only to give truthful answers to some such questions as the following: Does he get up in the morning by his own alarm clock, or
does someone have to call him repeatedly? Does he manage his
small weekly allowance with some discretion—make it last
through the week and occasionally save some of it for some major
purchase? Or is it all spent within the first day or two for trifling
indulgences? Does he on the whole choose his friends wisely, or
do Mother and Dad have to pry him loose every little while
from associates whom he should have been able himself to recognize as undesirable? And especially, when he has "home work"
to do, does he get at it himself and stay with it till it is done, or
does someone have to watch to see that he does not let it go and
slip out in the car or to the movies? If the answers to most of the
foregoing questions are favorable, the boy is probably ready for

college on the score of sufficient self-mastery. If the answer to a good many of them must be unfavorable, there is grave danger that he will encounter disaster in college, and if he were my boy I should not send him, irrespective of his intellectual brilliance— not yet.

There remains the difficult question as to what should be done with the boy or girl of college age who under the criteria presented above does not measure up to the college standard. The limits of this article permit only a summary and dogmatic answer to that question.

The answer depends, of course, upon which one or several of these criteria the youngster fails to meet. If the deficiency is in bookish aptitude, the college road should be definitely and permanently avoided. It can lead only to failure, discouragement, inferiority complexes, and personality maladjustments. In cases of special talent for music, art, or acting, not conjoined with bookish aptitude, I would strongly recommend one or more years in a conservatory, a school of art or design, or a school of dramatic art; this recommendation is based on the strictly educational consideration that, quite irrespective of whether the youngster finally makes a career of his talent, he will get in such a school much more real education and development, general as well as special, than he would in college. In other cases, where the parents can afford it—and it will cost no more in money than a year of failure in college—a trip abroad or around the world or a year on a western ranch is an educationally excellent temporary alternative. But in most cases, the alternative, immediately or shortly, is a job, in choosing which—even under our present economic stress—every effort should be made to see that it is in accordance with the boy's or girl's best aptitude, whatever that may be. For example, the boy with mechanical aptitude, but without the mathematical ability necessary for the profession of engineering, may well be encouraged to take a job in a garage or an electrical supply store, with a view to working up to the management of his own automobile or electrical business. And the boy with personal-relations **aptitude, but without bookish ability, should certainly go directly** into business, in which his success is as nearly certain as any success can be.

If the disqualifying deficiency is not in bookish aptitude but in intellectual interest or in self-mastery, the same answers hold good, except that in these cases they should be regarded as possibly temporary—not necessarily final. A year or two of additional maturity and practical experience will often see the emergence of one or more genuine intellectual interests. Even more frequently the discipline of a job for a year or two will develop an adequate degree of self-mastery. After such a flowering of genuine interest in studies, or such an attainment of capacity for self-direction, a young man or woman who would previously have entered upon an apathetic and profitless—or a highly checkered and equally profitless—four years, may then enter college with the prospect of real success.

Dying for "Dear Old ——" [1]

HEYWOOD BROUN

In appearance, Heywood Broun was untidy and unkempt. He weighed over two hundred pounds, let his hair grow like the lawn of a deserted house, and scuffled along without a vestige of polish on his size-thirteen shoes. "He always looked," a friend of his once said, "as if he had taken the coal out of the bathtub and then decided not to take a bath after all." This is the man who daily flaunted the bright pennant of his indignation in his column, "It Seems to Me," in the New York *World-Telegram*.

This enormous indifference to personal appearance may be a reaction to the days when Heywood Broun was a fat little boy in Brooklyn, dressed up in the Lord Fauntleroy tradition of velvet pants and long golden ringlets. The other boys used to call him "Christopher Columbus," and if he tried to fight, they seized a curl on either side and yanked. So the child shunned these harsh contacts, played by himself, and grew up into a shy and introspective young man.

After Harvard and a year of travel, Broun got a job on a New York newspaper, where he served without distinction until he was promoted to the post of baseball reporter. In this capacity he was in his element, for even then, Broun's writing had to be personal or it was of no worth. Here he could express his own opinions, shouting, praising, boisterously taking sides. He could build up and tear down reputations. All the glamour of the baseball diamond was his for the taking. He became the best all-round sporting writer of his time.

In 1917, Heywood Broun met and married Miss Ruth Hale, newspaper woman and president of the Lucy Stone League. The marriage attracted wide attention due to Miss Hale's insistence on the right to retain her own name. "A human being needs a name," her husband argued as he eloquently backed her up in her belief.

Broun's career as sports writer ended with his assignment to France as special war correspondent. He went into the trenches

[1] Reprinted by special arrangement with Heywood Broun.

with the first division of the American Expeditionary Forces, and saw fighting enough to make him a confirmed pacifist. Home again after the War, he worked on the *Tribune* as dramatic critic, and then on the *World*, all the time developing his powers of personal expression, proving his natural instinct for emotional and intellectual prodding. Then came his great chance—a column of his own. "It Seems to Me" became a daily feature of the New York *World*, with an increasing number of readers who enjoyed seeing its author tweak the noses of smug reformers, caricature the ardent efforts of censors, or in a milder mood, discourse on the virtues of owning a dog or being a father.

Heywood Broun wrote no verse to fill his column, invented no personages, but talked about himself and his opinions, and as he was not bothered by false reticences, his topics were numerous. On whatever subject, he said what he thought with vigor and with ease. He wrote in the simplest way, his distinction arose from the zest with which he hunted new ideas and from the skill with which he put them to work.

"Fired" from the *World* for expressing his opinions too freely, Broun took "It Seems to Me" to the *Telegram*. These two papers later became one after the sad demise of the *World*, and its assimilation by Mr. Roy Howard into his paper to form the *World-Telegram*. So "It Seems to Me" and the *World*, what was left of it, were together again.

The task of filling a column day in and day out, six days every week, was no simple assignment. It cannot be expected that every column was going to be good every day. But Broun's contributions always gave one unfailing impression—that he wrote easily and well. Besides filling his allotted newspaper space every day, Broun had eight books published; he staged and acted in two musical shows; he once made a strong but losing race for Congress on the Socialist ticket, and ever and anon he held an exhibition of his own paintings—interesting more for the running comments of the artist than for the quality of the art.

Franklin P. Adams, the F.P.A. of "The Conning Tower" fame, says of Heywood Broun:

"I was his office mate for eight or nine years on the *Tribune*, and for six years on the *World*. I saw him nearly every day during that time, and many nights. I had known him for years; come to think of it, I was best man at his wedding—the best, that is, that he could get on short notice—but I know little about him except a few facts. I cannot reduce them to their lowest terms for you, because Broun did not resolve into the ordinary prime factors of human relationships."

ـﭬ ـﭬ

A YOUNG man is being supported by two comrades as he limps across a field. It would not be stretching a point to call him a boy, as he is just past nineteen. His face is grimed and bloody and one foot drags behind him. He is crying. Not because of his injury, mind you, for this is a deeper hurt. A cause for which he has fought is going down to defeat. After the grave disaster of this afternoon his team has lost all claim to the football championship of Cambridge, New Haven, and Princeton, New Jersey.

He is young, you say, and will soon get over the tragedy which has come upon him. I am not so sure of that. I remember the man who dropped the punt during my freshman year at Harvard. Everybody thought Yale would win easily, but the Crimson line was holding beyond all expectations. The score was 0 to 0 and then this man came into the game. The first play to follow was a punt by the Yale fullback. This man had the ball squarely in his arms. He dropped it. Down flashed a Yale end and in six rushes the ball was carried over the line; there was no further scoring. Yale won.

All this happened in November, and in June there wandered about the yard an unhappy soul who was known to all his fellows as "the man who dropped the punt." He was a senior and it may be that graduation brought some release, although it must have been hard for him to find a spot in the United States to which the news of his mishap had never carried. Fate had been harsh to him but not unscrupulous, exactly. He did drop the punt. The true protagonist of the tragedy was another. He might have been spared, for at the time his brother dropped the punt this one had not yet matriculated at Harvard. That made no difference. The tradition endured. During his four years of college life he was known universally as "the brother of the man who dropped the punt."

And in all seriousness I advance the surmise that there are middle-aged men in this country who have been a little embittered and shaken for thirty years because of the fact that in some critical football game they acquitted themselves badly. The team on which they played was beaten.

I don't think this is a fantastic assumption. Unless he grows up to be President, or defendant in an important murder trial, the college football player is likely to receive far more extensive and searching newspaper publicity during his undergraduate days than at any other period of his life. He is called upon to face an emotional crisis in his life and to be watched by seventy thousand as he faces it. On the following day several million people will read of what he did. The quarterback who calls for a plunge through center will be publicly denounced as dull-witted if the play is piled up just short of the goal line. To stumble in the spotlight never did anybody any good, and if the man who falls happens to be nineteen years old he may get an ego bruise which will leave him permanently tender. And if he succeeds brilliantly he may be no better off. The American community is cluttered with ineffective young men who gave their souls to learn dropkicking and then found that there was no future in it.

The football player is not permitted to take any big game casually. Emotionalizing his men is accepted by the coach as a necessary part of his functions. "I was assigned to work on a big halfback," a former football star at Harvard told me. "He was a good defensive player but in the early games he didn't seem to show much fire. He was a lonely sort of fellow and it took me some time to find a line to get going on. We talked awhile and he told me that he came from Weston, Massachusetts. I said to him, 'My brother lives in Weston, and when you get in that game tomorrow I want you to play so that he and everybody else in Weston will be proud of you. You don't want to disgrace my brother in Weston, do you?'

"It was perfectly true that I did have a brother in Weston," my football friend continued, "and the angle I took worked all right. In fact it worked a little too well. After I'd been talking about Weston for quite a time this big halfback began to cry. I couldn't get him to stop. He was crying the next morning when we got out to the field and the doctor wouldn't let him attend the talk before the game. The doctor had to walk him up and down the sidelines to get him quieted down. Still he did go in and play a whale of a game."

I've always wanted to get an exact transcript of the parting words of a head coach to his men or his subsequent speech between the halves. I do know one but it was delivered to the squad of a comparatively small college. Just before the North Carolina eleven took the gridiron against Harvard their coach said to his players, "I want you boys to remember that every man on the Harvard team is a Republican."

But in this case oratory failed. The game was a conventional Republican landslide. More effective was an address delivered to another Southern team which invaded the North. On this occasion the coach relinquished his privilege of providing the last words and called an old gentleman into the locker room. And the voice of the veteran rang out like a trumpet call. He spoke of the Civil War and of how the South had held the Yankees back for four years. There was a line not to be split by any Yankee plunger. And the sons of Rebs could do it again. The old man called on the excited youngsters to remember Stonewall Jackson and Robert E. Lee. They remembered and played gloriously but later there was hard feeling, for the discovery was made that the old man had never served with any of the great commanders whom he mentioned but had actually marched with Sherman from Atlanta to the sea.

Coaches are fond of saying, "I want you boys to fight and to keep on fighting." If asked to explain his precise meaning the coach would undoubtedly answer with complete sincerity, "I told them to play hard." But it does not always work out that way. Only too often the instructions are taken all too literally. Football grows cleaner but Spotless Town is still a long march ahead. And when a young man deliberately injures an opposing player by the use of foul tactics there are accessories before the fact. Graduates who insisted loudly that "Dear Old ———" must have a winning team, and coaches who said that defeat would sully the honor of the institution, must share in the blame. It isn't possible to rouse impressionable youth right up to the point of being ready to die for "Dear Old ———" and not have a few of them, in the heat of battle, come to the decision that some of the foe ought at least to be maimed for the same good cause.

In spite of the stiff penalty provided by the rules, slugging continues. The officials can't see everything. Again and again players are tackled after they have crossed the sidelines and the whistle has blown. Men who are down get jumped upon. To be sure there is a difference between hard football and dirty football. When one watches the big games from way up on the rims of bowls and stadiums he is likely to have a good deal of trouble in detecting just where honest ardor ceases and the foul play begins. I have observed, however, that star players tend to get injured a little more often than those of slighter worth. To be sure, the burdens of attack and defense fall more frequently to the stars, but this is not the only reason. Football, even under strict observance of the rules, permits the practice of disarming the enemy by injuring his most conspicuous players.

And in addition to physically dirty play there are other devices not wholly glamorous. A great college coach taught his scrub team to curse the varsity players most foully through an entire week of practice. "It worked well," explained a veteran of that eleven. "When we got into the big game that Saturday I never paid any attention to the names they were calling me. I don't care about being called names like that, but the practice made me used to it. The coach told us not to listen to anything but the signals and to go through with our assignments. They did the cursing and we won the game."

And if all this is well founded, why is college football looked upon as the very flower and pattern of the highest sporting ideals in America? I don't know why. I like to watch college football and I can get emotional about it, but when I want moral stimulus and confirmation for my faith in the fundamental romanticism of man I go to see professional baseball. There have been scandals in the big leagues and even the most worthy and honest player is paid for his performances on the diamond. That doesn't matter. The distinction between the amateur and the professional cannot be reduced to a simple formula. In any field of endeavor your true and authentic amateur is a man who plays a game gleefully. I have never seen any college player who seemed to get half so much fun out of football as Babe Ruth derives from baseball. Ruth is able to contribute this gusto to his game spontaneously. Nobody makes him a set speech in the dressing room before he embarks to meet his test. The fans will not spell out "N–E–W Y–O–R–K" with colored handkerchiefs to inspirit him. There will be no songs about hitting the line. Indeed, Ruth will not even be asked to die for the cause he represents.

Instead of running out at top speed, Babe Ruth may be observed ambling quite slowly in the general direction of the diamond. He approaches a day's work. This thing before him is a job and it would not be fitting for him to run. But a little later you may chance to see a strange thing happen. The professional ball players take up their daily tasks. Soon, in the cause of duty, Ruth is called upon to move from right center all the way to the edge of the foul line. And now he is running. To the best of my knowledge and belief there is no current gridiron hero who runs with the entire earnestness of Ruth. Once I saw him charge full tilt against the wall of the Yankee Stadium. It was a low wall and Ruth's big body was so inextricably committed to forward motion that a wall was insufficient to quell the purpose inhering in the moving mass. And so his head and shoulders went over the barrier and, after a time, his feet followed. The resulting tumble must have been at least as vicious as any tackle ever visited upon a charging half-back. But for Ruth there was no possibility of time out. He could not ask so much as the indulgence of a sponge or a paper drinking cup. Shaking the disorders out of his spinning head, he tumbled himself back over the wall again and threw a runner out at the plate.

It is my impression that in the savage charge up to the wall and over, Ruth was wholly in the grip of the amateur spirit. If he had stopped short of the terrific tumble his pay would have still continued. To me there is nothing very startling in the fact that young men manage to commit themselves wholeheartedly to sport without hope of financial return. That is a commonplace. Recruiting volunteer workers for any cause is no trouble at all. I grow more sentimental over a quality much rarer in human experience. I give my admiration utterly to that man who can put the full sweep of effort into a job even though he is paid for it.

The bleeding right tackle making a last stand on the goal line is to me a lesser figure than Walter Johnson staving off the attack of the Giants in the final game of the World's Series. For, as I look at it, the bleeding tackle is fighting merely for the honor and glory of his college. My mind will not accept him as a satisfactory symbol of any larger issue. But when Johnson pitched I felt that the whole samurai [1] tradition was at stake. Once I shook hands with Walter Johnson and he remarked that the late summer had been a handicap for pitchers. Nothing more was said and I got no direct personal emanation from the man which convinced me that I was in the presence of true greatness. It never was the real Johnson but only the fictional one which captured my imagination. He was the Prince of Pitchers and the Strikeout King. From Montana he came to the big leagues to throw a baseball faster than it had ever been thrown before. And as a boy I read of how the hands of his catcher were bruised and maimed by the ordeal of receiving this mighty delivery.

And so Johnson became a demigod, and I am always sad when the gods die. I saw Johnson sicken under torture as the Giants scourged him. I watched him driven to the dugout in defeat. And then I saw him come back from his cavern revivified with all his old magic. This demigod was alive again and before me was

---

[1] *Samurai.* The fighting caste of Japan, an ancient and honored class bound by strict rules of personal and professional conduct.

playing out a solar myth. So it had been with Buddha and Osiris. There is resiliency in the soul of man and he may lie down to bleed awhile and return refreshed. College football is just a game; professional baseball can rise to the height of a religious experience.

And it is a religion with only the scantiest bonds of ritual. It is incumbent upon the faithful to stretch in the seventh inning. Beyond complying with that one easy ceremony, the rooter has no responsibility in this Quaker meeting. If he chooses to sit silent that is permissible. Only when the spirit truly summons him is there any necessity of shouting. And so I find the emotion of a big-league ball game far more genuine and deep-rooted than at any college football encounter. All shade and sensitivity are sacrificed in football by the pernicious practice of regimentation. "A long cheer with three 'Harvard's' on the end," cries the man in the white sweater through his megaphone. It is entirely possible that at the precise moments he calls upon me and my fellows to declare ourselves there is stored up in none of us more than a short cheer. It may even be that we have no inclination to cheer at all. Still, the duty is heavy upon us and we must render lip-service.

Before the afternoon is done the vilest sort of hypocrisy will be forced upon us. When the team in blue comes out upon the gridiron we shall all be called upon to render them a long cheer and to add three "Yale's" for courtesy. This is in violation of the deeper feelings of the human heart. We wish no success to Yale. At the mass meeting eloquent speakers have pointed out that it is imperative to the honor of Harvard that Yale shall be turned back from our gates. Already we have sung of our intention to smash, bleach, and ride them down. And here we are called upon to cheer them. It is all too distracting. Ambi-valency is not a condition which one cares to celebrate at the top of his voice.

The psychology of baseball is much more simple and more honest. The Washington rooter makes no pretense of wishing the Giants well. He pays them the compliment of thoroughgoing opposition. In the first game of the last World's Series two home runs were made by New York players. It was as if a lace handkerchief

had been tossed into the Grand Canyon. There was an aggressive
silence. A sincere horror and anguish struck forty thousand people
into a muteness which fairly throbbed. They made no dishonest
pretense of polite applause but maintained instead an honorable
silence.

And yet your baseball player and your baseball fan never take
defeat in any such tragic spirit as the football collegian. Finality is
so long delayed. The game which is lost may be cancelled by
victory on the succeeding day. And all this serves to create in the
mind of the impressionable a picture of life more accurate than
that which is conveyed by football. Defeat is a portion of every
man born into the world. He must learn to accept it and, if he is
to amount to much in his community, he must get from every
check a certain stimulus to appeal from the decision. There is no
use crying over spilt milk because it is no great trouble to run
around the corner and get another bottle. As our Salvation Army
friends say, "A man may be down but he's never out." That won't
do for a football proverb. A team can be both. Princeton, let us
say, has just run rings around Harvard. The final whistle has
blown. From this there can be no appeal. The issue may not be
tried again. The teams will not meet for another year and then
many a new figure will be in the lineup of either side. Here is a
finality which is disturbing. The Harvard rooters have no recourse
except to say that football is not so terribly important and that
anyway Harvard still has a better English department.

I arranged that my small son should first come into contact
with sport by watching professional baseball. One reason is wholly
unconnected with ethics. When he asks questions I am better prepared to answer them. But beyond that I don't want him to think
of a game as something which leaves two or three young men
stretched on their backs in the wake of every smashing play. I
cannot think up any good reason, suitable to his immature years,
why these young men should submit to such an ordeal. The chairman of the football committee at a great Eastern university
explained to a mass meeting that preparedness was the chief jus-
tification for intercollegiate football. He said that unless the young

men of America submitted to the arduous discipline and drill of training and the hard, fierce knocks of fighting football, we should have no adequate officers for our next war. But I don't want to use that reasoning on my small son. I have tried to enlist him in the determined ranks of those who insist that there will be no next war.

Only once did I ever hear of an official football speech which met with my entire approval. It was made by a Harvard captain. His team had lost to Yale but by a smaller score than was expected. It had been a fast and interesting game. At the dinner when the team broke training the captain said, "We lost to Yale but I think we had a satisfactory season. We have had fun out of football and it seems to me that ought to be the very best reason for playing the game."

A shocked silence followed his remarks. He was never invited to come to Cambridge to assist in the coaching of any future Harvard eleven. His heresy was profound. He had practically intimated that being defeated was less than tragic.

Personal Reactions

Hard Boiled [1]

ALBERT PAYSON TERHUNE

Albert Payson Terhune is best known as a writer of dog stories, and as owner of the kennels where the renowned "Sunnybank" collies are bred. But in the days before he won his fame and fortune, Mr. Terhune weathered a struggle such as many other young men have had to face. At the age of thirty-two, he was reporting for the New York *World* and trying to support a family on $47.50 a week. He was several thousand dollars in debt and faced with the possibility of losing his job.

Because he had to have more money he began writing fiction, working long hours after his day's job was done, and going without lunches to pay for having the material typed. His first story, a serial, he sold for $125, and from then on continued to market his yarns at increasingly higher prices. As his worries diminished, his ability increased, so that instead of losing his reporter's job he had his salary raised.

With a substantial, assured income, Mr. Terhune bought "Sunnybank," the home he now occupies at Pompton Lakes, New Jersey. The dogs he raises here are famous for their breeding and intelligence, and his stories about them are not only entertaining, but authentic. Mr. Terhune has not forgotten his early days of hardships which he refers to in "Hard Boiled," the essay which follows.

Albert Payson Terhune was born in Newark, New Jersey, in 1872. He is a graduate of Columbia University and has studied in Paris, Rome, and Geneva. His mother was Mary Virginia Terhune, an author of note, and his wife is Anice Stockton Terhune, who has many stories and musical compositions to her credit.

ᔐ ᔐ

HE WAS right disreputable in appearance. He had the look of being tied together with frayed strings. My only mental criticism of his attire, when he hove in sight, was that

[1] From *Proving Nothing*, by Albert Payson Terhune, published by Harper and Brothers. Reprinted by special arrangement with Harper and Brothers.

he looked *too* disreputable. There seemed too much artistic completeness to his get-up.

Six of us were coming down Broadway from a club dinner. The hour was 1 A.M.; the night was sloppy and chill. The derelict accosted us. I knew he was going to. Men sauntering along together in evening dress at that hour are rightly supposed to be mellow of mood—which is another way of saying they are generous.

"F'r Gawdsake, gents!" he croaked, hollowly, barring our way, "gimme a dime to save the wife and the baby from starving. Me, I don't care do I starve or don't I starve. I'd be better off dead than like this. It's them I'm praying to you for—for her and baby! F'r *Gawdsake!*"

There was a passion of appeal in the hoarse voice. It was aquiver with earnestness. But the loose mouth was placid. The eyes showed none of the sick dullness that goes with despair. His suit was picturesquely ragged, but his shoes had sound soles in spite of their tattered aspect, and their laces were new.

Also, though he wore no tie and had on a filthy shirt, yet the edge of his dirty collar was not frayed, nor had its points worn frayed spots on the shirt. His face was screwed into a doleful pucker. But under the eyes it was neither hollow nor dark, nor were there lines of hunger, or of fatigue, or of misery, at the mouth corners.

Now, I knew by experience that shoe laces break and need knotting long before a pair of shoes begins to fall apart. Nor do the shoes' uppers go before the soles. Also, the chief handicap to keeping up a decent appearance on an old and meager wardrobe is the fraying of collar edges. Next to that is the fraying of an old shirt from the constant rubbing of collar corners.

Long-sustained hunger or despair do subtle but readable things to the human face, if one has the wit to know how to detect them.

My five friends dug deep into their pockets and began exhuming silver pieces or small bills. They pressed these on the weepingly grateful derelict. Then they noticed that I alone had not swelled the collection.

"Broke?" one of them asked me, coldly.

"No," I made answer. "Just stingy."

"You can stand by and not raise a finger to keep a fellow man from starving?" demanded another, with booze-born fervor. "You can let his poor sick wife and his baby die of hunger? Thank Heaven, I'm not as hard boiled as you are!"

The rest echoed his virtuous tirade. Even the derelict glared at me in mute rebuke. The term "hard boiled" was repeated most often and most accusingly, of all the several reproving epithets launched at me by my indignant friends. The accusation was not new to me. I had been its recipient more than once. It did not seem to call for defense, so I made none. But as the derelict shuffled away with his handful of silver and bills I stopped him.

"You've got all you're going to get," I said. "So you can give yourself the luxury of telling the truth, for once. What are you going to do with the bunch of cash these saps have given you?"

For a moment he seemed about to burst forth into whiningly righteous indignation. Then perhaps he recognized in me a kindred soul, for he grinned up at me and said:

"If Judgment Day don't happen till I can walk to the nearest speak-easy, I'm going to get drunk."

No, I was not hard boiled. If I had been I should have turned him over to a policeman who came sauntering along the other side of the street. I should have had him punished by the law as an impostor. Instead of that, my heart warmed to the miserable chap's flash of impudence and I hurried the others along, lest they, too, see the policeman and want revenge for their lost money.

Which brings up an often-discussed question as to just what a man or woman must do or be in order to merit that hackneyed invective, "hard boiled."

In oviology, the difference between a three-minute egg and a thirty-minute egg is merely twenty-seven minutes, plus edibility and non-edibility. Applied to us humans, the two terms have perhaps two thousand differentiations.

Those five men thought I was hard boiled. The derelict branded the five at once as easy marks, and scorned them accordingly. I think the reason why so few people agree on the meaning of the phrase is because so few people recognize the vast difference between a hard-boiled brain and a hard-boiled heart.

Without a hard-boiled brain it is as difficult to go through life unsmashed as for a three-minute egg to go scatheless through a stone-crusher. A hard-boiled heart is a far different proposition. It is as much of a curse to its possessor as to those around him.

I am sentimental enough to believe that not one mortal in five hundred has a really hard-boiled heart. But a brain and a judgment that are not hard boiled are wont to become mushy and scrambled. Do you see the difference?

Not only in self-defense must the judgment be hard boiled, but sometimes out of kindness to others. The dentist who pulls your back tooth halfway out, and then stands weeping with sympathy for your sufferings, is far less kind to you than is the hard-boiled tooth-yanker who goes at his murderous job as quickly and as thoroughly as possible. It is so all through life.

A magazine editor gave me the following instance of the cruelty of being soft boiled at a time when the exercise of a thirty-minute-boiled brain would have been more merciful:

"Some months ago a man came to me," he said, "with some manuscripts to sell. I was courteous to him. Perhaps so courteous as to give him unconsciously the impression that I was an easy mark and that his manuscripts were already as good as sold to me. That is where I made my error.

"I read the manuscripts. They were impossible—at least for our magazine and, I think, for any other magazine of high standards. I had to tell him so. His face fell. He and his wife had come to New York to 'crash the gates of glory' and of literary success. They had not done well in the uphill fight for recognition.

"Then, when I was courteous to him and seemed sympathetic with his efforts, his hopes had run high. He and his wife had believed that the long period of probation was ended and that they had 'arrived.' They celebrated their coming triumph by treating themselves to a party or two that they couldn't afford. Then the blow fell.

"The husband declared I had misled him as to his stories' chances. I had not intended to mislead him at all. I had felt sorry for him and so I had tried to show him I would give him every possible consideration his work deserved. He mistook this for a sure sale. I would have been kinder if I had been hard boiled with him from the start.

"A friend asked me, as a favor, to read a manuscript written by an acquaintance of his. I ought to have been hard boiled enough to say, 'No, I have enough manuscripts to read in the course of my daily work. I won't take the trouble to read this one.' I consented to read it. I had one of our magazine's fiction readers go through it, too, and then I tried to get a literary agent to sell it to some publisher.

"In all, I must have given a full day's time to the thing a full day outside of my regular working hours. My task was in vain. The novel—so far as I have heard—never sold. My reward was that its author's wife has been telling people, more or less publicly, that I stole the plot of her husband's book and that I sold the story, thinly disguised, for my own gain.

"Both of these times, I should have been hard boiled, and I wasn't. Both times it would have been kinder. Both times I wasted time and labor, and made enemies by doing it."

Unquestionably, life would run smoother and more pleasantly, all around, if everybody knew just when to be hard boiled. Think, for a moment, of a few gorgeous things that would happen:

If I dared to go into a barber shop, get my shave and hair cut and facial massage and shampoo and manicure, and get my boots blacked and my clothes brushed, and then pay the checks and walk out without giving an extra penny to barber or boot-black or manicure or brush boy—think of the cash I'd save, and the self-respect as well!

If I had the sublime hard-boiledness to go into a restaurant and eat and pay for a meal and then go out leaving the waiter tipless and without giving a grudged and unearned coin to the hat boy or hat girl ——!

Suppose everyone was hard boiled enough to do these and similar heroic but supremely common-sensible things? Don't you see what would happen? Well, among other results, we should all be far richer at the end of the year, and we should be richer, too, in the knowledge that we had not cringed in cowardly guise to pay undeserved cash-tribute.

Also, barbers and waiters would serve all customers alike and not neglect a small-tip patron for a slinger of huge tips. Their tyrannical power would be gone. The hat-check girl or boy would have to go to work, somewhere, for a living, and might in time become a worth-while member of the human race, instead of an itching-palmed parasite.

Most of the petty nuisances of life would dissolve under the brave sanity of a worldful of thirty-minute human eggs!

And, mind you, that would be a case of hard-boiled brain and judgment, not of hard-boiled heart. None of those people and others of their kind—barbers, hat-checkers, waiters, red-caps, Pullman porters, taxi-drivers and the like—none of them are objects of charity. We tip them through cowardice, not from generosity. All are getting fair pay for their work—or all would get it if their employers did not trade on the soft-boiledness of patrons to eke out the employees' wages. If we did not tip, the employer would have to pay better money to these and other workers. We are not helping them. We are helping him.

You did not give a quarter to the man who sold you the necktie you bought today or a five-dollar bill to the clerk who sold you a ticket from New York to Chicago, nor a penny tip to the bus or trolley conductor. But custom says you must pay it to barber and taxi-man and waiter, etc. So, being soft boiled in judgment, you pay it. (So do I, to my shame.)

The truly hard-boiled-brained man is the sworn, if unconscious, enemy to "bunk" in all its myriad forms. And if he be consistently hard boiled, he does not lose popularity by it, in the long run, for half the world trades on the soft-boiledness of the other half.

The string that is twanged on hardest and oftenest is our sense of the pathetic. Hence the avalanches of hard-luck stories that precede each "touch." Steady of mind is he who can go through life listening to an endless succession of these hard-luck tales without losing his own faith in the inherent squareness and sweetness of human nature.

Sentimental gush and hard-luck stories—how many hundred million dollars, I wonder, have they wheedled out of folk who could not afford to pay so high a price for the privilege of listening to such slush!

I am not talking about cases of true charity, where the heart is involved and where your hard-boiled mind tells you to yield to your soft-boiled heart and to go to the rescue. I am speaking of the traditional and chronic and worthless hard-luckers and sentimentalists. The only possible armor against such a bombardment is a thirty-minute-boiled judgment.

And it works inversely, too. A mighty weapon in the hand of an employer is the appeal to his workers' soft-boiled side, whether for extra toil or a temporary cut in pay, out of loyalty to the dear old firm, or by the testimonial dinner wherewith a long-service employee is rewarded. This latter is, to me, one of the most pitiful impositions of the lot.

John Jones has been working for the Ironsoul Pump Corporation from the time he entered the place as a twelve-year-old office boy until his scanty hair has grayed through fifty years of stanch laboring for his boss's betterment.

Mr. Ironsoul is reminded that Jones has worked for him for a half-century. Something ought to be done. Besides, here is a chance for a bit of free newspaper advertising. Ironsoul turns the matter over to his secretary with instructions. Presently word runs around the works that a semi-centennial dinner is to be tendered to good old John Jones of the export division, and that the boss will appreciate it if department heads and seconds-in-command will attend. (Tickets $3.50, except to John Jones, who for once gets something free.)

Jones sits at the right hand of the boss, while several hand-picked speakers tell him how fine he is and how lucky to work for such a firm. Ironsoul himself pays him a high tribute and winds up with glowing eloquence about the beauties of loyalty. If enough has been subscribed, Jones may even be presented with a very thin silver loving-cup, rendered unpawnable by reason of the mass of engraved lettering on it.

Jones goes home that night, carrying the cup (or the handsomely engrossed vellum testimonial, if enough cash was not raised to buy a cup at wholesale rates), and he has a choky feeling in his throat as he remembers the wonderful things the Big Boss said about him. It makes up to him for his half-century of grinding toil—his Golden Wedding to grim Labor—and it is lucky it *does* make up to him; for that is all the poor old cuss has to show for his fifty years of loyalty and sweat.

The hard-boiled boss has put it all over the soft-boiled wage slave. Now if Jones had had a thirty-minute-boiled brain, he would have spoken somewhat as follows when the Big Boss broke the news to him about the testimonial banquet:

"Mr. Ironsoul, that is a first-rate idea. I've got it coming to me, along with a lot of more worth-while things. I've saved you many thousands of dollars in my day. I stood by you, at low wages, during the three panic years when you were almost down and out. I stopped that strike of the puddlers, eighteen years back. I showed you, several times, how to save big wads of money, by minor efficiency stunts I had worked out.

"I've done all this and a lot more. I've been loyal to you. *But just remember that when loyalty is all on one side, it stops being loyalty and becomes servility.* In view of my record, I am glad to accept the dinner. And I am sure you'll make announcement during the evening that you are taking that occasion to present me with three hundred shares of your company stock or with a substantial pension of some other kind, as a slight recognition of my long and valuable service.

"I can't do you the injustice to believe that you are trying to get away with your tremendous debt to me by tendering me nothing more than just a measly dinner and a twenty-five-dollar silver cup. So in advance I thank you for the pension. Without it the dinner would be a cruel practical joke."

Does Jones say that? And does his employer come across? If so, it never gets into the papers, though I have read a score of items telling of just such dinners to faithful old workers.

Employers are, and ever have been, prone to reward faithful service in some such cleverly futile way. A few years ago a play, *To the Ladies*, summed up this hard-boiled trait far better than I can. The president of a great piano company was speaking at the annual dinner of his office-and-factory force. I quote from his oration:

"It has long been the hope of the Company to do something for its loyal employees—something in recognition of the services they have given. I am glad to announce that that moment is at hand and that our employees, particularly those who have been with us for some years, are to be recognized.

"Beginning January first, every man who has been with the Company five years or more will be entitled to" (here a pause, and breathless eagerness from the hearers)—"will be entitled to wear a button—a solid silver button. . . . We feel that money is a poor return for loyalty. So we have devised this little silver button which will be marked by one gold stripe for each five years of service."

Could anything be more sublimely and yet more smoothly and adamantly hard boiled? I'll wager that *that* company never went into involuntary bankruptcy and that the directors never were saddened by a request to approve a pension.

Then here is another instance (a true one, and not culled from a clever play, like the foregoing) of something we were speaking about earlier in this article—the dangerous folly of not being hard boiled enough at any given time.

A man who worked on the same newspaper with me, some quarter-century ago, could have won any office prize for 100 per cent unpopularity. Everyone loathed him. At last came the glad word that he had accepted a job on another paper and in another city. It seemed almost too good to be true.

Instead of sitting tight, in safe hard-boiledness, members of the staff were so grateful to him for going away that they gave him a farewell dinner. This same rejoicing at the prospect of losing him made the evening's speakers praise him highly and say that his departure would gloom the whole office.

In the midst of these laudatory and regretful speeches, he arose and left the room. Three minutes later he came back, aglow with happiness. Addressing the assemblage he shouted:

"Did you boys think I'd really leave the dear old paper, now that I know how you all feel about me? I was only going because I thought I wasn't liked. Now that I know how much I'm loved by all of you, I'm going to stay as long as I live. I've just sent a telegram, refusing my new job. Any man would be an idiot to leave a staff where he's so popular."

And stay he did, thanks to our exhibition of soft-boiled brains.

When you go to your tailor and merely order two suits at most, does he never intimate to you that a man with any sort of claim to good grooming ought to have at least twelve business suits? And if he does intimate that, aren't you sometimes soft boiled enough to increase your original order? Not to twelve suits, per-haps, but to one or two more than you need or had intended to buy? Have you the hard-boiled nerve to say to him:

"That is an old wheeze that you shears-and-cloth pirates have agreed on among yourselves. It's no business of yours whether I choose to have twelve suits or one, or if I prefer to run around in a horse blanket. Now shut up and measure me for what I have ordered and for nothing more. Get busy."

If you said that, the tailor could not have you put into jail or even expelled from any of your clubs. He couldn't do a thing and he wouldn't do a thing. He would not even refuse to measure you. In his heart would dawn a certain respect for you. But you dare not do it. (Neither do I.)

Instead, you shuffle about and mutter something about having been hit pretty hard on Wall Street lately, and that by and by you intend to get a number of suits, etc.

It is the same along all lines of fashion. Sapphire Smith looked like a Misfortune, when she adopted skirts to the knees and a shingle bob, a few years ago. She is one of the women to whom a long dress and coils of soft hair are tremendously becoming. They give her her only claims to beauty and to distinction. Did she dare wear them? If so, I have not chanced to meet her, nor one woman in a thousand who has the hard-boiledness to defy the various commands of fashion for the sake of individual attractiveness.

A straw hat is a cool and usually a becoming head covering for men. During certain arbitrarily-decreed months in summer a man may wear one. The last half of September may be, and often is, piping hot. But what man is so hard boiled as to go forth into the streets on September 29th—or any time after mid-September—wearing straw headgear? A hot felt hat on a hot September day is his badge of three-minuteness.

But we were speaking of hard-boiledness as an armor. It is, and often a highly needful one. Many years ago, for instance, I worked in an office whose city editor was known through all other offices of the same profession as the Simon Legree of journalism. He was a brute. That is the mildest thing to be said of him. Let's call him Smithers.

One of his workers—Brown will do for a name—died. Brown had had hard luck for some years. He left a wife and two small children, and he left nothing else. They were destitute.

Some of us got up a subscription for the widow and children. One of us took it to Smithers, sullenly unwilling to brave a rebuff from the hated boss, but still more unwilling to rob Mrs. Brown and her children of any off chance of getting an extra dollar or so. Smithers glanced at the subscription list, then thrust it from him.

"I won't give a penny to save the whole lot of them from the poorhouse!" he snarled. "It isn't my fault the poor fool hadn't sense enough to save his money. I'm no easy mark."

We collected what we could. One of the men took the small offering to the widow. She thanked him. Then, bursting into tears she exclaimed:

"And oh, may God bless Mr. Smithers for all his wonderful goodness!"

Our emissary blinked foolishly. This sounded like wild irony. He inferred that she thought the collection was a personal gift from her husband's Simon Legree boss, and he began to seek words to undeceive her. But she continued, breathlessly:

"Mr. Smithers came right up here, himself, the minute he heard of my loss. No father could have been more tender or more consoling to me than he was. He said such beautiful things about my poor husband! Then he made me give him the funeral bill, and he wrote out a check for it, and he gave me five hundred dollars more, to go on with."

That is all there is to the story. It is true. And it illustrates, more clearly than could a bookful of my own clumsy writing, the difference between the hard-boiled brain and the hard-boiled heart.

Smithers, as I learned afterward, did things of that kind again and again. But if the office had known of it, he would have been assailed by myriad hard-luck stories. He would have been pestered for undeserved raises of salary and he would have been begged to subscribe to every senseless object in all the eternal succession of a newspaper office's quasi-charities. Thus he wore the only armor that could possibly have protected him.

More than once I have known of men of enormous wealth coupling their several-figure subscriptions to some worthy cause by making the gift contingent on strict secrecy. This not only through modesty, but to shield themselves against the army of begging letters and hard-luck-story sentimentalists who would have rushed to the feast at first hint that a new victim had been discovered.

Yet I believe every hard-boiled armor contains a wide chink through which a rightly-aimed shaft of appeal can be shot deep into the soft-boiled heart. I have found innumerable instances of it.

The late J. P. Morgan was notoriously hard boiled. He was adamant to a swarm of money-suckers who tackled him from every angle. But——

A group of reporters sat around a table in Lipton's café on Nassau Street, in the glad old days before Prohibition came—and went. One of them was broke and out of work. He had the promise of a job the following week, but he had no cash to tide him over or to get out of pawn the only decent suit he owned.

Calling for pen and paper, he scribbled a jolly little tale of his woes—an audacious and non-whining request for fifty dollars—and sent it to J. P. Morgan's office by a messenger boy. He did it as a joke. He did not know Morgan. Morgan had never heard of him. But Morgan chanced to be the first rich man whose name he thought of. Expecting nothing, he wrote gaily and rather brilliantly.

Twenty minutes later the messenger boy came back to Lipton's and handed the reporter the envelope in which he had sent his letter to the financier. It contained a fifty-dollar bill. No word of writing, but just the money. By some rare good luck the reporter had chanced to strike a weak spot in the Morgan armor.

By the way, that story went all over newspaperdom. No fewer than a hundred more or less needy reporters sprained their intellects to write similar jocose appeals to Morgan. To the best of my knowledge not one of them received any kind of reply.

Bob Fitzsimmons, once champion heavyweight prize-fighter of the world, was equally hard boiled. Here is a tale of him told me by Fred Leighton, the collie breeder. Both men are dead now. Said Leighton:

"I landed in America, down and out. I had met Bob Fitzsimmons in the old country. I called on him and asked him to lend me ten dollars and to let me work it out in some way. He answered that he was no soft spot, and that he wouldn't lend a penny to anyone. He was insulting in his manner and he bawled me out as a dead beat, and then he told me to leave his house.

"I went away smarting from his rotten treatment of me. My eyes stung, and I took out my handkerchief to wipe them. With the handkerchief, out rolled ten ten-dollar bills that Fitzsimmons had stuck there as he went to the front door with me.

"I ran back to thank him. He told me I was crazy and that

he hadn't done anything of the kind. He said he'd knock my block off if I tried to spread such a fool story about him. Six months later I had saved enough from a job to pay back his hundred dollars. I took the money to him and he wouldn't touch it. He still kept insisting he hadn't given me a penny."

Yet Bob Fitzsimmons had a reputation for "nearness," even in the heyday of his fortune and fame! To have been known as lending money to the needy would have swamped him with fake suppliants. Hard-boiled head, soft-boiled heart.

Speaking of the chinks in our hard-boiled armor, I think we all have them. I have at least two. I am slightly ashamed of them both. Moreover, they are nobody's business but my own, and I have no intention of letting myself in for a flood of begging letters—I get quite enough already—by confessing what they are.

A man admitted to me, once, that though he could yawn in the face of a weeper, yet if an applicant could make him laugh he became all at once soft boiled. Another said to me:

"There are only three things in all the world that can smash through my armor. All three of them are a frightened little child, crying."

Personally, if I want any favor I would rather ask it of a hot-tempered man who begins the interview by being cranky. Loss of temper always lays open a man's armor chinks. The man who is calmly and smilingly sure of himself is a terrible foe to the seeker of such chinks. A smiling calmness seems to be the trademark of the thoroughly hard boiled. I envy it—when it is genuine. It implies self-sureness—a glorious quality. Of an American general it was said by a member of his staff:

"He is the most even-tempered man in the army. He is mad all the time."

Obviously, the general was one man who was anything but sure of himself.

I have heard more than once the query, "But why do we need to be hard boiled?"

The answer is very simple: Because the world is organized largely on the principle of getting something from the other fellow. People are forever trying to sell you something you don't want or need. People are forever wanting you to do or to give something that you don't want to do or give.

The man with the soft-boiled brain or with a brain not hard boiled enough to counterbalance his soft-boiled heart, is certain to be stung, fore and aft, and to be victimized. In order to carry a brain and judgment competent to fend off these pests (and to guard against one's unwise impulses) it is necessary to be hard boiled.

There are many definitions of hard boiled, most of them signifying heartlessness. I do not think any of them is correct. Perhaps I am not correct, myself, in my own idea of what is meant by the word. Here is my definition of it. Take it or leave it:

To be hard boiled means to be so certain of yourself that it makes no difference to you what other people may do or say or think.

I was a bit proud of this until I repeated it to a woman who is wise. She thought a minute, then replied:

"Why, isn't that the definition of pig-headedness?"

Perhaps it is. But who ever heard of a pig that was fooled or imposed on or victimized (during his lifetime) or was coaxed into doing something his own common sense and his own wishes did not approve of? There are far stupider and worse treated animals than the pig.

If your hard-boiledness makes you unfair to humanity at large or unkind to those who have a just claim on your tenderness, then it is a vice; and it is not the thing which I have here been praising.

It should be the mosquito netting which you wear for protection when you change the location of beehives. It should not be a bludgeon to shatter the hives to pieces and harm their occupants.

In other words, it should be used as a defensive, not an offensive weapon; to guard its owner from a million troubles that beset him on every hand, not to make the world less happy and less comfortable for others.

And shan't we remember to keep it all in the brain where it

belongs and let none of it seep down into the heart, where it has no place?

Perhaps I have not made so great a success of my own efforts to do this that I can afford to preach it to others. But it is a grand idea, none the less.

Reading and Writing

Clamming

ARCHIBALD MacMECHAN

Archibald MacMechan, the son of Rev. John MacMechan, was born in Kitchener, Ontario, in 1862. Upon completing his primary and secondary schooling at Picton Union school and Hamilton College he came to the University of Toronto. After graduation he was appointed as teacher of Modern Languages at Galt Collegiate Institute for the year 1885-86. He spent the following three years at Johns Hopkins University. From there he went to Dalhousie University at Halifax, Nova Scotia, where he taught until his retirement more than forty years later. He remained actively interested in Canadian education and literature until his death in 1933. Among his best known works may be listed *Red Snow on Grand Pré*, *There Go the Ships* and *Old Province Tales*.

᳐᳐   ᳐᳐

De profundis clamavi

THE scene is far too grand for the trivial action staged upon it. In front is the North Mountain; behind is the Basin. Between, on the vast red clay foreshore left bare by the ebb, is a solitary human figure. It is the Summer Boarder engaged in clamming. The crest and flanks of the long trap-rock wall called North Mountain are clothed with spruce forest. At its feet stand white farm-houses amid green orchards and greener fields of oats. There are no fences to be seen; but lines of low bushes give the impression of English hedgerows. Fifteen miles away the parallel wall of South Mountain shows like a low-lying bank of faint blue cloud. The horizon is beset all round with snowy, puffed cloud masses which cannot climb higher. From the center of the immense, aëry dome, dwarfing the whole landscape, the sun pours midsummer radiance and genial heat. The colours are green and red—green of a hundred shades, orchard and oat-field and grassland and potato-patch—red of sandy beach and earthy cliff carved and worn by countless tides. But the Summer Boarder has eyes for none of these things; he is intent on clamming.

Clamming may be defined as the art or science of extricating the clam from his native mud. The process sounds extremely simple. There is the mud in which the clam lies embedded a few inches below the surface. Here is the hunter armed with a narrow shovel or a five-pronged stable fork. The clam must passively abide your onset. He cannot run away; he cannot fly in the air. You assail him with your digging implement. Insert it at the right place, turn over the mud, and there is the clam ready to hand over to Mrs. Cook for the chowder or the stew.

But there is always a difference between theory and practice; clam-digging is not without its difficulties. The quarry must first be tracked to his lair. His "spoor" is the tiny spiraculum, or blow-hole, which the clam makes in the mud. The larger the blow-hole, the larger the clam, say the natives, a saying which experience does not invariably confirm. Below this the clam lies *perdu* with his long, thick—proboscis, shall we call it?— extended at full length outside the two valves of his shell. This is the "tough end," which serves as a handle to dip him into the melted butter of the clam-bake banquet. It is not eaten. Where the "spoor" is plenty, it is safe to thrust in your fork. Returns are fairly certain if not quick.

The prior question of equipment for the chase must not be hastily dismissed as unimportant; for every form of field sport has its appropriate accoutrement. There be those who hunt the clam in rubber boots. A bathing-suit is far better. Failing this, the clam-hunter is well advised who pursues his game collarless, coatless, barefoot, with rolled-up shirt-sleeves and double-reefed trousers. For he will see a new meaning in the old question, "What costume should a lady wear in a mud-bath?" Clam-hunting is bathing in mud. The clam-hunter comes into most intimate relations with primeval slime; he cannot but remember the pit from which he was dug; he becomes of the earth, earthy; he achieves a condition of miry slushfulness which Mr. Browning's Caliban might envy. "Sans armor," as far as possible, let the clam-hunter take the field. Washing up thereafter will take less time.

It might be assumed that the odds are all against the quarry; but the clam has a sporting chance for his life, at least against such an amateur as the present writer. Digging for clams in midsummer is no child's play. The clay is a stiff compound of glue and putty. Turning it over with a superannuated shovel is toil comparable to ditching. The shovel is soon clogged with thick lumps of clay, which must be scraped off before a second thrust can be made. It is slow, heavy work. Even when the right quarter section is overturned, and the clam should be revealed in his burrow, he may escape in the turmoil of ooze and water. The ratio has not been worked out; but probably ten shovelfuls of heavy clay are lifted and shifted for every clam dropped into the bucket. Even when the operation is successful, disappointment may follow. The clam may be too small to add to your collection and must be put back to grow. The process of filling the bucket is slow and toilsome; but the labour only sharpens the appetite and makes the clam more thoroughly appreciated when he fulfils the end for which he was created and comes to the table as the chief ingredient of a savoury bakemeat.

The psychology of the clam has no doubt been exhaustively studied, but possibly the observations of an independent investigator (who has dug for clams twice or thrice ere now) may not be altogether without value. The world has a low opinion of the clam's mentality. In common parlance, clam is synonymous with fool; and indeed he is the Nabal of bivalves; folly remaineth with him. Why else should he reveal his presence to his human enemy by spouting thin jets of water through his proboscis? A truly wise beast like the oyster or the mussel remains passive and undemonstrative at the approach of danger. The clam would seem to be of a nervous, excitable temperament. The approach of the spade compressing his muddy home apparently angers or frightens him, and he spouts in a sort of hysterical fury. Can it be that he thinks he is defending himself by putting out the rash beholder's eye? Or insulting him by spitting in his face? The popular advice not to be a clam is justified by the observed facts.

The happiness of the clam, especially at high water, has also passed into a proverb. Perhaps it is because he is a fool that he is happy in his unreflecting way. Pessimism and *Weltschmerz* have passed him by. Of course, at high water the clam is safe from his human enemies, which may be the ground for his rejoicing.

Finis coronat opus. At last the bucket is filled. A little stream that pursues its own course across the sands makes a convenient wash-hand basin. The reward of the persistent clammer looms near. Supper is no longer a far-off divine event. Presently he will sit down to the table with tranquil nerves, braced muscles, and even-flowing blood; before him will steam the soup-plate of ambrosia called chowder; he will forget the toilsome spade and the heavy clay; he will think only of the comfortable creature which tastes as no purchased or market clam could possibly taste.

From *The Book of Ultima Thule*, by Archibald MacMechan. Used by permission of the publishers, McClelland and Stewart Ltd., Toronto.

Theme Writing [1]

DOROTHY CANFIELD FISHER

Dorothy Canfield was born in the small college town of Lawrence, Kansas, in 1879, into surroundings which offered unusual
intellectual stimulus. Her mother was an artist and her father
was then president of the University of Kansas. Her early education was acquired in such diverse settings as her mother's studio
in the Latin Quarter of Paris, French convent schools, and Ohio
State University. She has a Ph.D. from Columbia, and has
traveled and lived in various foreign countries. Learning languages is her pastime.

In 1907, Dorothy Canfield married John Redwood Fisher, a
writer and critic. They have two children. Early in the War,
Mr. Fisher joined an ambulance corps in France, and very soon
after, Mrs. Fisher followed him there. Placing her children in a
Paris school, she gave all her time and energies to war relief,
aiding soldiers blinded in battle, looking after refugees, and caring
for orphans. The results of her war experiences are related in her
collections of short stories, *Home Fires in France* and *The Day of
Glory*, two of her finest books.

Back home after the War, the Fishers resumed their normal
mode of living. A true cosmopolite, Mrs. Fisher scorns any veneer
of smug sophistication, and chooses as her permanent home an
ancestral farmhouse on a Vermont hill, and as her pattern of
conduct a high ideal of work and service. They travel extensively,
in America and abroad, wanting for their children the wide out-
look which results from knowing how other people live.

Mrs. Fisher writes of the things she knows, and always her
characters are endowed with her own high standards. Her best
work is found in her novels, among them *The Bent Twig*, *Her Son's
Wife*, *The Brimming Cup*. She is almost equally proficient as a short-
story writer, while her essays, if not so numerous, show in striking
manner the clearness of thought which is one of her outstanding
characteristics.

[1] Reprinted by special permission of Dorothy Canfield Fisher.

SCIENTISTS tell us it is harder to start a stone moving than to keep it going after it gets started. And every writer can bear witness that the most unyielding stone is mobile as thistledown compared to the inertia of the average human mind confronted with a blank sheet of paper.

It is hard to write. It is infinitely harder to begin to write. Don't I know it? I have been earning my living by my pen for twenty-five years. I shouldn't like to guess how many hundred thousand words I've put on paper, and I have never in my life sat down at my desk and started off without hesitation, repugnance, and wild flounderings. Other authors confess that it is much the same with them. There are exceptions—stories, even novels, where the opening words pop right into one's mind, part of the first conception, but these inspirations are far between.

I set down all this not to discourage those of you who are wondering if perhaps it might not be possible to become an author, still less to add to the gloom of wrestling with the English compositions you all have to write. On the contrary, I hope to encourage you by letting you know that those hopeless moments of inhibition before the blank page, those chewed, balky penholders are only the common lot. There is nothing the matter if you can't start writing without effort. Nobody can.

But perhaps this sounds a little bit like the fortune teller who predicted, "You will have forty years of bad luck and then—then you will be used to it." It is not so bad as that. It is quite true that no one ever learns to write both well and easily. But there are tricks to every trade and some of the most useful of them all are ways of tricking your own rebellious nerves. Perhaps it would help you to know of one that works with most writers. Whenever they have a piece of writing to do, *they begin to write*—to write something, anything. They conquer the inertia of their minds by a spasm of effort, just as a man might give a great heave to a boulder that blocks his way. Grimly, doggedly, they keep on writing. Often what they are setting down is flat, stale balderdash, and they know it. No matter! If they are experienced writers they keep right on, do not stop—not to sharpen a pencil, or get a drink of water, or go to look out of the window, although they yearn to do all these things. They have learned by experience that if they sit and stare at the paper they are lost. The rosy, hazy half-thoughts which flit about the back of the mind always vanish when one tries to think them out. The only way to catch them is to put down on the paper as many of them as possible.

So the struggling author plods ahead, filling page after page with horrible, unwieldy sentences, haphazard, unleavened ideas, and after a time it begins to move more smoothly. Is it because of habit, or because the subconscious mind wakes up, or is it something similar to physical momentum? Nobody knows, but it almost always works. The great boulder begins to roll evenly and more and more in the desired direction. Apter phrases suggest themselves. The whole subject begins to take on shape. Even now it is not good. But there is something there, some stuff which can later be licked into shape. Then comes the moment when the writer realizes that he has said somehow all that was in his mind.

The work is far from being finished, but the hardest part is over. Now comes the mechanical task of breaking up ungainly sentences, cutting out the flat words and phrases, thinking up colorful ones to fill the gaps, shifting related ideas into paragraphs. It is a matter of skill and judgment, only a little harder than correcting grammatical errors—far different from the agony of trying to create, or rather to drag out the raw material from the fringe of consciousness.

It is mechanical work but very necessary. Inexperienced writers don't do enough of it. Very young writers often do not revise at all. Like a hen looking at a chalk line, they are hypnotized by what they have written. "How can it be altered?" they think. "That's the way it was written." Well, it has to be altered. You have to learn how. That is chiefly what English classes can teach you. They can't give you thoughts and material to write about. Only your inherited brain cells and the enriching experience of life as you live it can do that. But you can learn to put what material you have into form. In manual training you wouldn't hand in a lot of sticks and boards bunched together with string, and call it a table. It's no better to hand in a detached bundle of statements, starting nowhere in particular, trailing along a while and then fading out—and call it a theme.

All your first drafts will need revision, but the middle and end of them may not need a great deal. You had steam up when you wrote them; you were commencing to feel what you wanted to say. But *watch your beginning*. That was written when arm and brain were cold. Try as you may to put it into shape, the first page or so is generally hopeless. Then cut it out and begin where the real life begins. You may hate to sacrifice that laboriously written first page, but if it isn't right, can't be made right, it isn't worth keeping. When you wrote it you were only warming up your arm. Do that behind the grand stand, and when you start the game be ready to pitch real ball.

(The following paragraphs describe Mrs. Fisher at work on one of her stories, "Flint and Fire.")

The story was now ready to write.

I drew a long breath of mingled anticipation and apprehension, somewhat as you do when you stand, breathing quickly, balanced on your skis, at the top of a long white slope you are not sure you are clever enough to manage. Sitting down at my desk one morning, I "pushed off" and with a tingle of not altogether pleasurable excitement and alarm, felt myself "going." I "went" almost as precipitately as skis go down a long white slope, scribbling as rapidly as my pencil could go, indicating whole words with a dash and a jiggle, filling page after page with scrawls . . . it seemed to me that I had been at work perhaps half an hour, when someone was calling me impatiently to lunch. I had been writing four hours without stopping. My cheeks were flaming, my feet were cold, my lips parched. It was high time someone called me to lunch.

The next morning, back at the desk, I looked over what I had written, conquered the usual sick qualms of discouragement at finding it so infinitely flat and insipid compared to what I had wished to make it, and with a very clear idea of what remained to be done, plodded ahead doggedly, and finished the first draft before noon. It was almost twice too long.

After this came a period of steady desk work, every morning, of rewriting, compression, more compression, and the more or less mechanical work of technical revision, what a member of my family calls "cutting out the 'whiches.' " The first thing to do each morning was to read a part of it over aloud, sentence by sentence, to try to catch clumsy, ungraceful phrases. . . . Always interwoven with these mechanical revisions were recurrent intense visualizations of the scenes. This is the mental trick which can be learned, I think, by practice and effort. Personally, although I never used as material any events in my own intimate life, I can write nothing if I cannot achieve these very definite, very complete visualizations of the scenes; which means that I can write nothing at all about places, people, or phases of life which I do not intimately know. If my life depended on it, it does not seem to me I could possibly write a story about Siberian hunters or East-side factory hands without having lived long among them.

Now the story was what one calls "finished," and I made a clear copy, picking my way with difficulty among the alterations, the scratched-out passages, and the cued-in paragraphs, the inserted pages, the rearranged phrases. As I typed, the interest and pleasure in the story lasted just through that process. But on taking up the legible typed copy and beginning to glance rapidly over it, I felt fall over me the black shadow of that intolerable reaction which is enough to make any author abjure his calling forever. By the time I had reached the end, the full misery was there, the heart-sick, helpless consciousness of failure. . . .

From the subconscious depths of long experience came up the cynical, slightly contemptuous consolation, "You know this never lasts. You always throw this same fit, and get over it."

And sure enough, the next morning, after a long night's sleep, I felt quite rested, calm, and blessedly matter-of-fact. "Flint and Fire" seemed already very far away and vague, and the question of whether it was good or bad, not very important or interesting, like the chart of your temperature in a fever now gone by.

In Foreign Places

Views of Holland

ALDOUS HUXLEY

Aldous Huxley was born on July 26, 1894. He is the grandson of Thomas H. Huxley, the well-known writer, and the son of Leonard Huxley, LL.D., formerly editor of the *Cornhill Magazine*. Aldous was educated at Eton and at Balliol College, Oxford. During his college days he wrote a number of pieces of poetry; his first complete work, *The Burning Wheel*, was published in 1916.

The subsequent works of Aldous Huxley include *The Defeat of Youth and Other Poems* (1918); *Crome Yellow* (1921); *On the Margin* (1923); *Essays New and Old* (1926); *Point Counter Point* (1928); *Beyond the Mexique Bay* (1934).

In 1919 he married Maria Nys, a native of Belgium. During the following year he was Dramatic Critic on the *Westminster Gazette*. His own opinion of this experience can be described most aptly in his own words:

> "Once, in the course of an ill-spent life, it was my fate to go to the theatre some two hundred and fifty times in one year. On business, I need not add; one would hardly do that sort of thing for pleasure. I was paid to go.

> "By the end of the year—and, for that matter, long before our planet had completed its orbit round the sun—I had come to the conclusion that I was not paid enough; that, indeed, I could never be paid enough for this particular job. I gave it up; and nothing would now induce me to resume it."

Aldous Huxley has travelled widely during his life; he has visited this Dominion, the West Indies, Guatemala, Mexico, Japan and Burma and has also spent a considerable time in Europe. The charm of the essay which follows has thus been enhanced both by the wide personal experiences of the author and by his consequent ability to present only those elements of his subject which make it worthy of descriptive treatment. In it Huxley writes about Holland from two points of view,—points of view which differ from each other mentally if not physically.

As you read the essay, try to discover what aspects of the country make the greatest appeal to the author, at all times noting the point of view from which he is describing his subject.

∽ ∽

I HAVE always been rather partial to plane geometry; probably because it was the only branch of mathematics that was ever taught me in such a way that I could understand it. For though I have no belief in the power of education to turn public school boys into Newtons (it being quite obvious that, whatever opportunity may be offered, it is only those rare beings desirous of learning and possessing a certain amount of native ability who ever do learn anything), yet I must insist, in my own defence, that the system of mathematical instruction of which, at Eton, I was the unfortunate victim, was calculated not merely to turn my desire to learn into stubborn passive resistance, but also to stifle whatever rudimentary aptitude in this direction I might have possessed. But let that pass. Suffice to say that, in spite of my education and my congenital ineptitude, plane geometry has always charmed me by its simplicity and elegance, its elimination of detail and the individual case, its insistence on generalities.

My love for plane geometry prepared me to feel a special affection for Holland. For the Dutch landscape has all the qualities that make geometry so delightful. A tour in Holland is a tour through the first books of Euclid. Over a country that is the ideal plane surface of the geometry books, the roads and the canals trace out the shortest distances between point and point. In the interminable

From *Essays New and Old*. Copyright, 1927, by George H. Doran Company. Reprinted by special arrangement with Aldous Huxley, Doubleday, Doran and Company, and James B. Pinker and Son, Inc.

polders, the road-topped dykes and gleaming ditches
intersect one another at right angles, a criss-cross of perfect
parallels. Each rectangle of juicy meadowland contained
between the intersecting dykes has identically the same
area. Five kilometres long, three deep — the figures record
themselves on the clock face of the cyclometer. Five by
three by — how many? The demon of calculation possesses
the mind. Rolling along those smooth brick roads between
the canals, one strains one's eyes to count the dykes at right
angles and parallel to one's own. One calculates the area
of the polders they enclose. So many square kilometres.
But the square kilometres have to be turned into acres. It
is a fearful sum to do in one's head; the more so as one
has forgotten how many square yards there are in an acre.

And all the time, as one advances the huge geometrical
landscape spreads out on either side of the car like an
opening fan. Along the level sky-line a score of windmills
wave their arms like dancers in a geometrical ballet. In-
eluctably, the laws of perspective lead away the long roads
and shining waters to a misty vanishing point. Here and
there — mere real irrelevancies in the midst of this ideal
plain — a few black and white cows out of a picture by
Cuyp browse indefatigably in the lush green grass or, remembering Paul Potter, mirror themselves like so many
ruminating Narcissi, in the waters of a canal. Sometimes
one passes a few human beings, deplorably out of place,
but doing their best, generally, to make up for their ungeometrical appearance by mounting bicycles. The circular
wheels suggest a variety of new theorems and a new task
for the demon of calculation. Suppose the radius of the
wheels to be fifteen inches; then fifteen times fifteen times
pi will be the area. The only trouble is that one has forgotten the value of *pi*.

Hastily I exorcise the demon of calculation that I may be
free to admire the farmhouse on the opposite bank of the

canal on our right. How perfectly it fits into the geometrical scheme! On a cube, cut down to about a third of its
height, is placed a tall pyramid. That is the house. A
plantation of trees, set in quincunx formation, surrounds it;
the limits of its rectangular garden are drawn in water on
the green plain, and beyond these neat ditches extend the
interminable flat fields. There are no outhouses, no barns,
no farm-yard with untidy stacks. The hay is stored under
the huge pyramidal roof, and in the truncated cube below
live, on one side the farmer and his family, on the other
side (during winter only; for during the rest of the year
they sleep in the fields) his black and white Cuyp cows.
Every farmhouse in North Holland conforms to this type,
which is traditional, and so perfectly fitted to the landscape
that it would have been impossible to devise anything more
suitable. An English farm with its ranges of straggling
buildings, its untidy yard, full of animals, its haystacks and
pigeon-cotes, would be horribly out of place here. In the
English landscape, which is all accidents, variety, detail
and particular cases, it is perfect. But here, in this general-
ized and Euclidean North Holland, it would be a blot and
a discord. Geometry calls for geometry; with a sense of the
æsthetic proprieties which one cannot too highly admire,
the Dutch have responded to the appeal of the landscape
and have dotted the plane surface of their country with
cubes and pyramids.

Delightful landscape! I know of no country that it is
more mentally exhilarating to travel in. No wonder
Descartes preferred the Dutch to any other scene. It is the
rationalist's paradise. One feels as one flies along in the
teeth of one's own forty-mile-an-hour wind like a Cartesian
Encyclopædist — flushed with mental intoxication, convinced that Euclid is absolute reality, that God is a mathematician, that the universe is a simple affair that can be
explained in terms of physics and mechanics, that all men

are equally endowed with reason and that it is only a
question of putting the right arguments before them to
make them see the error of their ways and to inaugurate the
reign of justice and common sense. Those were noble and
touching dreams, commendable inebriations! We are
soberer now. We have learnt that nothing is simple and
rational except what we ourselves have invented; that God
thinks in terms neither of Euclid nor of Riemann; that
science has "explained" nothing; that the more we know
the more fantastic the world becomes and the profounder
the surrounding darkness; that reason is unequally distrib-
uted; that instinct is the sole source of action; that prejudice is incomparably stronger than argument, and that even
in the twentieth century men behave as they did in the
caves of Altamira and in the lake dwellings of Glastonbury.
And symbolically one makes the same discoveries in Holland. For the polders are not unending, nor all the canals
straight, nor every house a wedded cube and pyramid, nor
even the fundamental plane surface invariably plane. That
delightful "Last Ride Together" feeling that fills one as
one rolls along the brick-topped dykes between the canals
is deceptive. The present is not eternal; the "Last Ride"
through plane geometry comes to a sudden end — in a
town, in forests, in the sea coast, in a winding river or great
estuary. It matters little which; all are fundamentally
ungeometrical; each has power to dissipate in an instant
all those "paralogisms of rationalism" (as Professor
Rougier calls them) which we have so fondly cherished
among the polders. The towns have crooked streets
thronged with people; the houses are of all shapes and
sizes. The coast-line is not straight nor regularly curved,
and its dunes or its dykes (for it must be defended against
the besieging waves by art if not by nature) rear themselves
inexcusably out of the plane surface. The woods are
unscientific in their shady mysteriousness and one cannot

see them for all their individual trees. The rivers are tortu-
ous and alive with boats and barges. The inlets of the sea
are entirely shapeless. It is the real world again after the
ideal — hopelessly diversified, complex and obscure; but,
when the first regrets are over, equally charming with the
geometrical landscape we have left behind. We shall find
it more charming, indeed, if our minds are practical and
extroverted. Personally, I balance my affections. For I
love the inner world as much as the outer. When the outer
vexes me, I retire to the rational simplicities of the inner —
to the polders of the spirit. And when, in their turn, the
polders seem unduly flat, the roads too straight and the laws
of perspective too tyrannous, I emerge again into the
pleasing confusion of untempered reality.

And how beautiful, how curious in Holland that confusion is! I think of Rotterdam with its enormous river and
its great bridges, so crowded with the traffic of a metropolis
that one has to wait in files, half a mile long, for one's turn
to cross. I think of The Hague and how it tries to be
elegant and only succeeds in being respectable and upper
middle class; of Delft, the commercial city of three hundred
years ago; of Haarlem where, in autumn, you see them
carting bulbs as in other countries they cart potatoes; of
Hoorn on the Zuyder Zee, with its little harbour and sea-
ward-looking castle, its absurd museum filled with rich
mixed rubbish, its huge storehouse of cheeses, like an old-
fashioned arsenal, where the workmen are busy all day long
polishing the yellow cannon balls on a kind of lathe and
painting them bright pink with an aniline stain. I think of
Volendam — one line of wooden houses perched on the
sea-wall, and another line crouching in the low green fields
behind the dyke. The people at Volendam are dressed as
for a musical comedy — *Miss Hook of Holland* — the men in
baggy trousers and short jackets, the women in winged
white caps, tight bodices, and fifteen superimposed petti-

coats. Five thousand tourists come daily to look at them;
but they still, by some miracle, retain their independence
and self-respect. I think of Amsterdam; the old town, like
a livelier Bruges, mirrors its high brick houses in the canals.
In one quarter an enormous courtesan sits smiling at every
window, the meatiest specimen of humanity I ever saw.
At nine in the morning, at lunch-time, at six in the afternoon, the streets are suddenly filled with three hundred
thousand bicycles; every one, in Amsterdam, goes to and
from his business on a pair of wheels. For the pedestrian as
well as for the motorist it is a nightmare. And they are all
trick cyclists. Children of four carry children of three on
their handle-bars. Mothers pedal gaily along with month-
old infants sleeping in cradles fastened to the back carrier.
Messenger boys think nothing of taking two cubic metres
of parcels. Dairymen do their rounds on bicycles specially
constructed to accommodate two hundred quart bottles of
milk in a tray between the two wheels. I have seen nursery
gardeners carrying four palms and a dozen of potted chrys-
anthemums on their handle-bars. I have seen five people
riding through the traffic on one machine. The most daring
feats of the circus and the music hall are part of the quo-
tidian routine in Amsterdam.

I think of the dunes near Schoorl. Seen from a little distance across the plain they look like a range of enormous
mountains against the sky. Following with the eye that
jagged silhouette one can feel all the emotions aroused,
shall we say, by the spectacle of the Alps seen from Turin.
The dunes are grand; one could write a canto from *Childe
Harold* about them. And then, unfortunately, one realizes
what for a moment one had forgotten, that this line of
formidable peaks is not looking down at one from fifty
miles away, over the curving flank of the planet: it is just
a furlong distant, and the chimneys of the houses at its base
reach nearly two-thirds of the way to the top. But what

does that matter? With a little good will, I insist, one can
feel in Holland all the emotions appropriate to Switzerland.

Yes, they are grand, the dunes of Schoorl and Groet. But
I think the grandest sight I saw in non-geometrical Holland
was Zaandam — Zaandam from a distance, across the plain.

We had been driving through the polders and the open
country of North Holland. Zaandam was the first piece of
ungeometrical reality since Alkmaer. Technically, Zaandam is not picturesque; the guide-book has little to say
about it. It is a port and manufacturing town on the Zaan,
a few miles north of Amsterdam; that is all. They make
cocoa there and soap. The air at Zaandam is charged in
alternative strata with delicious vapours of molten chocolate and the stench of boiling fat. In wharves by the shores
of the river they store American grain and timber from the
Baltic. It was the granaries that first announced, from a
distance, the presence of Zaandam. Like the cathedrals of
a new religion, yet unpreached, they towered up into the
hazy autumn air — huge oblongs of concrete set on end,
almost windowless, smooth and blankly grey. It was as
though their whole force were directed vertically upwards;
to look from windows horizontally across the world would
have been a distraction; eyes were sacrificed to this upward
purpose. And the direction of that purpose was emphasized
by the lines of the alternately raised and lowered panels into
which the wall spaces of the great buildings were divided —
long fine lines of shadow running up unbrokenly through
a hundred feet from base to summit. The builders of the
papal palace at Avignon used a very similar device to give
their castle its appearance of enormous height and formidable impendence. The raised panel and the shallow blind
arches, impossibly long in the leg, with which they varie-
gated the surface of the wall, impart to the whole building
an impetuous upward tendency. It is the same with the
grain elevators at Zaandam. In the haze of autumnal

Holland I remembered Provence. And I remembered, as I watched those towering shapes growing larger and larger as we approached, Chartres and Bourges and Reims: gigantic silhouettes seen at the end of a day's driving, towards evening, against a pale sky, with the little lights of a city about their base.

But if at a distance Zaandam, by its commercial monuments, reminds one of Provençal castles and the Gothic cathedrals of France, a nearer view proclaims it to be unequivocally Dutch. At the foot of the elevators and the only less enormous factories, in the atmosphere of chocolate and soap, lies the straggling town. The suburbs are long, but narrow; for they cling precariously to a knife-edge of land between two waters. The houses are small, made of wood and gaudily painted; with gardens as large as tablecloths, beautifully kept and filled — at any rate at the season when I saw them — with plushy begonias. In one, as large, in this case, as two tablecloths, were no less than fourteen large groups of statuary. In the streets are men in wooden shoes, smoking. Dogs drawing carts with brass pots in them. Innumerable bicycles. It is the real and not the ideal geometrical Holland, crowded, confusing, various, odd, charming. . . . But I sighed as we entered the town. The "Last Ride Together" was over; the dear paralogisms of rationalism were left behind. It was now necessary to face the actual world of men — and to face it, in my case, with precisely five words of Dutch (and patois at that) learned years before for the benefit of a Flemish servant: "Have you fed the cat?" No wonder I regretted the polders.

Jungle Night [1]

WILLIAM BEEBE

Beebe's accounts of his scientific explorations read like an improbable, thrilling, and beautiful adventure story. Through all his writings runs the feeling of exhilaration which he finds in his work. As a scientist, he performs his labors with tremendous precision and diligence, keeping voluminous notes. But his writing is in a spirit of relaxation, suiting his subject to his mood.

Beebe's voyages occupy from five to ten months of the year, and take him anywhere from British Guiana to the Hudson Gorge, or the bottom of a tropic ocean. He is charmed by the beauties of the bottom of the sea. "Don't die," he beseeches us, "without having borrowed, stolen, or purchased, or made, a helmet, to glimpse for yourself this new world."

William Beebe thinks that, removed from his work, he is of no interest whatsoever. But that belief is not shared by others, who find him enormously interesting. He was born in Brooklyn, New York, in 1877. He was graduated from Columbia University in 1898. Beebe is a tall man, standing six feet; he is slim, vigorous, enthusiastic, and looks at least ten years younger than he is. He likes New York for six months of the year—parties, dancing, the theater. He enjoys flying an airplane and driving an automobile. But more than everything else in the world, he likes his work. He considers it the most satisfying occupation on earth. Mr. Beebe is Director of Tropical Research of the New York Zoölogical Society and is the leading American authority on tropical birds. He cannot imagine a more horrible fate than to be without work.

William Beebe's books include: *Jungle Peace, The Edge of the Jungle, Jungle Days, The Arcturus Adventure, Pheasant Jungles, Beneath Tropic Seas, Nonsuch: Land of Water.*

ᔕ᠎   ᔕ

WITHIN gunreach in front of me trudged my little Akawai Indian hunter. Jeremiah was his civilized name; he would never tell me his real one. It seemed so unsuited to him that I

[1] From *Jungle Peace*, by William Beebe, published by Henry Holt and Company. Reprinted by special arrangement with William Beebe.

thought up one still less appropriate and called him Nupee—which is the three-toed sloth; and in his quiet way he saw the humor of it, for a more agile human being never lived. I knew Nupee for what he was—the one for whom I am always on the lookout, the exceptional one, the super-servant, worthy of friendship as an equal. I had seen his uncle and his cousins. They were Indians, nothing more.

Nupee and I had not been thrown together closely. This had proved a static expedition, settled in one place, with no dangers to speak of, no real roughing it, and we met only after each hunting trip. But the magic of a full moon had lured me from my laboratory table, and here we were, we two, plodding jungleward, becoming better acquainted in silence than I have often achieved with much talk.

It was nearly midnight. We traversed a broad trail of white sand, between lines of saplings of pale-barked rubber trees, flooded, saturated, with milky-gray light. Not a star appeared in the cloudless sky, which, in contrast to the great silver moon plaque, was blue-black. These open sandy stretches, so recently etched into what had been primitive jungle, were too glowing with light for most of the nocturnal creatures who, in darkness, flew and ran and hunted about in them. And the lovers of twilight were already come and gone. The stage was vacant save for one actor—the nighthawk of the silvery collar, whose eerie *wheeoo!* or more leisurely and articulate *who-are-you?* was queried from stump and log.

Where the open trail skirted a hillside we came suddenly upon a great gathering of these goatsuckers, engaged in some strange midnight revel. Usually they roost and hunt and call in solitude, but here at least forty were collected on the white sand within an area of a few yards. We stopped and watched. They were dancing—or, rather, popping, as corn pops in a popper. One after another, or a half dozen at a time, they bounced up a foot or two from the ground and flopped back, at the instant of leaving and returning uttering a sudden, explosive *wop!* This they kept up unceasingly for the five minutes we gave to them, and our passage interrupted them for only a moment. Later we passed single birds which popped and wopped in solitary state; whether practicing, or snobbishly refusing to perform in public, only they could tell. It was a scene not soon forgotten.

Suddenly before us rose the jungle, raw-edged, with border zone of bleached, ashamed trunks and lofty branches white as chalk, of dead and dying trees. For no jungle tree, however hardy, can withstand the blasting of violent sun after the veiling of emerald foliage is torn away. As the diver plunges beneath the waves, so, after one glance backward over the silvered landscape, I passed at a single stride into what seemed by contrast inky blackness, relieved by the trail ahead, which showed as does a ray of light through closed eyelids. As the chirruping rails climbed among the roots of the tall cat-tails out yonder, so we now crept far beneath the level of the moonlit foliage. The silvery landscape had been shifted one hundred, two hundred feet above the earth. We had become lords of creation in name alone, threading our way humbly among the fungi and toadstools, able only to look aloft and wonder what it was like. And for a long time no voice answered to tell us whether any creature lived and moved in the tree tops.

The tropical jungle by day is the most wonderful place in the world. At night I am sure it is the most weirdly beautiful of all places outside the world. For it is primarily unearthly, unreal; and at last I came to know why. In the light of the full moon it was rejuvenated. The simile of theatrical scenery was always present to the mind, the illusion lying especially in the completeness of transformation from the jungle by daylight. The theatrical effect was heightened by the sense of being in some vast building. This was because of the complete absence of any breath of air. Not a leaf moved; even the pendulous air roots reaching down their seventy-foot plummets for the touch of soil did not sway a hairbreadth. The throb of the pulse set the rhythm for one's steps. The silence, for a time, was as perfect as the breathlessness. It was a wonderfully ventilated amphitheater; the air was as free from any feeling of tropical heat, as it lacked all crispness of the north. It was exactly the temperature of one's skin. Heat and cold were for the moment as unthinkable as wind.

One's body seemed wholly negligible. In soft padding moccasins and easy swinging gait close behind my naked Indian hunter, and in such khaki browns that my body was almost invisible to my own downward glance, I was conscious only of the play of my senses—of two at first, sight and smell; later, of hearing. The others did not exist. We two were unattached, impersonal, moving without effort or exertion. It was magic, and I was glad that I had only my Akawai for companion, for it was magic that a word would have shattered.

At last the silence was broken and I stood in a patch of moonlight listening to the baying of a hound, or so I thought: that musical ululation which links man's companion wolfward. Then I thought of the packs of wild hunting dogs, the dreaded "warracabra tigers," and I turned to the Indian at my elbow, full of hopeful expectation. With his quiet smile he whispered, "*kunama*," and I knew I had heard the giant tree frog of Guiana—a frog of size and voice well in keeping with these mighty jungles. I knew these were powerful *beenas* with the Indians, tokens of good hunting, and every fortunate *benab* would have its dried mummy frog hung up with the tail of the giant armadillo and other charms. Well might these batrachians arouse profound emotions among the Indians, familiar as they are with the strange beings of the forest. I could imagine the great goggle-eyed fellow sprawled high near the roof of the jungle, clutching the leaves with his vacuum-cupped toes. The moonlight would make him ghostly— a pastel frog; but in the day he flaunted splashes of azure and green on his scarlet body.

At a turn in the trail we squatted and waited for what the jungle might send of sight or sound. And in whispers Nupee told me of the big frog *kunama* and its ways. It never came to the ground, or even descended part way down the trees; and by some unknown method of distillation it made little pools of its own in deep hollows and there lived. And this water was thick like honey and white like milk, and when stirred became reddish.

Besides which, it was very bitter. If a man drank of it, forever
after he hopped each night and clasped all the trees which he
encountered, endlessly endeavoring to ascend them and always
failing. And yet, if he could once manage to reach a pool of
kunama water in an uncut tree and drink, his manhood would
return and his mind be healed.

When the Indians desired this *beena*, they marked a tree
whence a frog called at night, and in the daytime cut it down.
Forming a big circle, they searched and found the frog, and forth-
with smoked it and rubbed it on arrows and bow before they
went out. I listened gravely and found it all fitted in with the
magic of the night. If an Indian had appeared down the trail,
hopping endlessly and gripping the trunks, gazing upward with
staring eyes, I should not have thought it more strange than the
next thing that really happened.

We had settled on our toes in a low squatting place—a dark
aisle with only scattered flecks of light. The silence and breathlessness of the moon craters could have been no more complete
than that which enveloped us. My eye wandered from spot to
spot, when suddenly I began to think of that great owl-like goat-
sucker, the *"poor-me-one."* We had shot one at Kalacoon a month
before and no others had called since, and I had not thought of
the species again. Quite without reason I began to think of the
bird, of its wonderful markings, of the eyes which years ago in
Trinidad I had made to glow like iridescent globes in the light
of a flash, and then—a *poor-me-one* called behind us, not fifty feet
away. Even this did not seem strange among these surroundings.
It was an interesting happening, one which I have experienced
many times in my life. It may have been just another coincidence.
I am quite certain it was not. In any event it was a Dantesque
touch, emphasized by the character of the call—the wail of a lost
soul being as good a simile as any other. It started as a high, trembling wail, the final cry being lost in the depths of whispered woe:

Oo———ooh! oh! oh! oh! oh! oh!

Nupee never moved; only his lips formed the name by which he
knew it—*halawoe*. Whatever else characterized the sounds of the

jungle at night, none became monotonous or common. Five minutes later the great bird called to us from far, far away, as if from another round of purgatory—an eerie lure to enter still deeper into the jungle depths. We never heard it again.

I was about to rise and lead Nupee farther into the gloom when the jungle showed another mood—a silent whimsy, the humor of which I could not share with the little red man. Close to my face, so near that it startled me for a moment, over the curved length of a long narrow caladium leaf, there came suddenly two brilliant lights. Steadily they moved onward, coming up into view for all the world like two tiny headlights of a motor-car. They passed, and the broadside view of this great elater was still absurdly like the profile of a miniature tonneau with the top down. I laughingly thought to myself how perfect the illusion would be if a red tail light should be shown, when to my amazement a rosy red light flashed out behind, and my bewildered eyes all but distinguished a number! Naught but a tropical forest could present such contrasts in such rapid succession as the *poor-me-one* and this parody of man's invention.

I captured the big beetle and slid him into a vial, where in his disgust he clicked sharply against the glass. The vial went into my pocket and we picked up our guns and crept on. As we traversed a dark patch, dull gleams like heat lightning flashed over the leaves, and, looking down, I saw that my khaki was aglow from the illuminated insect within. This betrayed every motion, so I wrapped the vial in several sheets of paper and rolled it up in my handkerchief. The glow was duller but almost as penetrating. At one time or another I have had to make use of all my garments, from topee to moccasins, in order to confine captives armed with stings, beaks, teeth, or fangs, but now I was at a complete loss. I tried a gun barrel with a handkerchief stopper, and found I now carried an excellent, long-handled flashlight. Besides, I might have sudden use for the normal function of the gun. I had nothing sufficiently opaque to quench those flaring headlights, and I had to own myself beaten and release him. He spread his wings and flew swiftly away, his red light glowing derisively; and even in the flood of pure moonlight he moved within an aura which carried far through the jungle. I knew that killing him was of no use, for a week after death from chloroform I have seen the entire interior of a large insect box brilliantly lighted by the glow of these wonderful candles, still burning on the dead shoulders of the same kind of insect.

Twice, deeper in the jungle, we squatted and listened, and twice the magic silence remained unbroken and the air unmoved. Finally it was lifted, however, as a sudden tearing rush from the rail side, and ripping of vines and shrubs, was mingled with deep, hoarse snorts, and we knew that we had disturbed one of the big red deer—big only in comparison with the common tiny brown brockets. A few yards farther the leaves rustled high overhead, although no breath of wind had as yet touched the jungle. I began a slow, careful search with my flashlight, and, mingled with the splotches and specks of moonlight high overhead, I seemed to see scores of little eyes peering down. But at last my faint electric beam found its mark and evolved the first bit of real color which the jungle had shown—always excepting the ruby tail light. Two tiny red globes gleamed down at us, and as they gleamed, moved without a sound, apparently unattached, slowly through the foliage. Then came a voice, as wandering, as impersonal as the eyes —a sharp, incisive *wheeeeeat!* with a cat-like timbre; and from the eyes and voice I reconstructed a night monkey—a *kinkajou*.

Then another notch was slipped and the jungle for a time showed something of the exuberance of its life. A paca leaped from its meal of nuts and bounced away with quick, repeated pats; a beetle with wings tuned to the bass clef droned by; some giant tree cricket tore the remaining intervals of silence to shreds with unmuted wing fiddles, *cricks* so shrill and high that they well-nigh passed beyond the upper register of my ear out again into silence. The roar of another frog was comforting to my eardrums.

Then silence descended again, and hours passed in our search for sound or smell of the animal we wished chiefest to find—the giant armadillo. These rare beings have a distinct odor. Months of work in the open had sharpened my nostrils so that on such a trip as this they were not much inferior to those of Nupee. This sense gave me as keen pleasure as eye or ear, and furnished quite as much information. The odors of city and civilization seemed very far away: gasoline, paint, smoke, perfumery, leather—all these could hardly be recalled. And how absurd seemed society's unwritten taboo on discussion of this admirable, but pitifully degenerate sense! Why may you look at your friend's books, touch his collection of *netsukés*, listen to his music, yet dare sniff at naught but his blossoms!

In the open spaces of the earth, and more than anywhere in this conservatory of unblown odors, we come more and more to appreciate and to envy a dog's sensitive muzzle. Here we sniffed as naturally as we turned ear, and were able to recognize many of our nasal impressions, and even to follow a particularly strong scent to its source. Few yards of trail but had their distinguishable scent, whether violent, acrid smell or delectable fragrance. Long after a crab jackal had passed, we noted the stinging, bitter taint in the air, and now and then the pungent wake of some big jungle bug struck us like a tangible barrier.

The most tantalizing odors were the wonderfully delicate and penetrating ones from some great burst of blossoms, odors heavy with sweetness, which seeped down from vine or tree high overhead, wholly invisible from below even in broad daylight. These odors remained longest in memory, perhaps because they were so completely the product of a single sense. There were others too, which were unforgettable, because, like the voice of the frog, they stirred the memory a fraction before they excited curiosity. Such I found the powerful musk from the bed of leaves which a fawn had just left. For some reason this brought vividly to mind the fearful compound of smells arising from the decks of Chinese junks.

Along the moonlit trail there came wavering whiffs of orchids, ranging from attar of roses and carnations to the pungence of carrion, the latter doubtless distilled from as delicate and beautiful blossoms as the former. There were, besides, the myriad and bewildering smells of sap, crushed leaves, and decaying wood; acrid, sweet, spicy, and suffocating, some like musty books, others recalling the paint on the Noah's Ark of one's nursery.

But the scent of the giant armadillo eluded us. When we waded through some new, strange odor I looked back at Nupee, hoping for some sign that it was the one we sought. But that night the great armored creatures went their way and we ours, and the two did not cross.

Finally we turned and circled through side trails so narrow and so dark that we walked with outstretched arms, feeling for the trunks and lianas, choosing a sloth's gait and the hope of new adventures rather than the glare of my flash on our path. When we entered the Convict Trail, we headed toward home. Within sight of the first turn a great black limb of a tree had recently fallen across the trail in a patch of moonlight. Before we reached it, the branch had done something it should not have done—it had straightened slightly. We strained our eyes to the utmost but could not, in this eerie light, tell head from tail end of this great serpent. It moved very slowly, and with a motion which perfectly confounded our perception. Its progress seemed no faster than the hour hand of a watch, but we knew that it moved, yet so close to the white sand that the whole trail seemed to move with it. The eye refused to admit any motion except in sudden shifts, like widely separated films of a motion picture. For minute after minute it seemed quiescent; then we would blink and realize that it was two feet higher up the bank. One thing we could see —a great thickening near the center of the snake; it had fed recently and to repletion, and slowly it was making its way to some hidden lair, perhaps to lie motionless until another moon should silver the jungle. Was there any stranger life in the world?

Whether it was a giant bushmaster or a constrictor, we could not tell in the diffused light. I allowed it to go unharmed, for the spell of silence and the jungle night was too strongly woven to be shattered again by the crash of gun or rifle. We waited for many minutes at the edge of the small glade, and the event which seemed most significant to me was in actual spectacle one of the last of the night's happenings. I sat with chin on knees, coolie fashion, in the white light of the glade. I watched the motionless leaves about me, many of them drooping and rich maroon by daylight, for they were just unbudded. Reaching far into the dark mystery of the upper jungle stretched the air roots, held so straight by gravity, so unheeding of the whirling of the planet through space. Only one mighty liana—a monkey ladder—had revolted against this dominance of the earth's pull and writhed and looped upon itself in fantastic whorls, while along its length rippled ever the undulations which mark this uneasy growth, this crystallized St. Vitus plant.

A momentary shiver of leaves drew our eyes to the left, and we began to destroy the optical images evolved by the moon shadows and to seek for the small reality which we knew lived and breathed somewhere on that branch. Then a sharp crack like a rifle lost whatever it was to us forever, and we half leaped to our feet as something swept downward through the air and crashed length after length among the plants and fallen logs. The branches overhead rocked to and fro, and for many minutes, like the aftermath of a volcanic eruption, came a shower, first of twigs and swirling leaves, then of finer particles, and lastly of motes which gleamed like silver dust as they sifted down to the trail. When the air cleared I saw that the monkey ladder had vanished and I knew that its yards upon yards of length lay coiled and crushed among the ferns and sprouting palms of the jungle floor. It seemed most fitting that the vegetable kingdom, whose silence and majesty gave to the jungle night its magic qualities, should have contributed this memorable climax.

Long before the first Spaniard sailed up the neighboring river, the monkey ladder had thrown its spirals aloft, and through all the centuries, all the years, it had seen no change wrought beneath it. The animal trail was trod now and then by Indian hunters, and lately we had passed several times. The sound of our guns was less than the crashing fall of an occasional forest tree. Now, with no leaf moved by the air, with only the two of us squatting in the moonlight for audience, the last cell had given way. The sap could no longer fight the decay which had entered its heart; and at the appointed moment, the moment set by the culmination of a greater nexus of forces than our human mind could ever hope to grasp, the last fiber parted and the massive growth fell.

In the last few minutes, as it hung suspended, gracefully spiraled in the moonlight, it had seemed as perfect as the new-sprouted *moras* at my feet. As I slowly walked out of the jungle I saw in this the explanation of the simile of artificial scenery, of all the strange magic which had come to me as I entered. The alchemy of moonlight turned all the jungle to perfect growth, growth at rest. In the silvery light was no trace of gnawing worm, of ravening ant, or corroding fungus. The jungle was rejuvenated and made a place more wonderful than any fairyland of which I have read or which I have conceived. The jungle by day, as I have said—that, too, is wonderful. We may have two friends, quite unlike in character, whom we love each for his own personality, and yet it would be a hideous and unthinkable thing to see one transformed into the other.

So with the mist settling down and tarnishing the great plaque of silver, I left the jungle, glad that I could be far away before the first hint of dawn came to mar the magic. Thus in memory I can always keep the dawn away until I return.

And some time in the future, when the lure of the full moon comes, and I answer, I shall be certain of finding the same silence, the same wonderful light, and the waiting trees and the magic. But Nupee may not be there. He will perhaps have slipped into memory. And if I find no one as silently friendly as Nupee, I shall have to watch alone through my jungle night.

Concerning Women

What a Young Girl Should Know [1]

Unlike the proverbial old maid who always knew just how to
raise other people's children, Mrs. Banning has had practical experience with young people's problems. She is the mother of two
children, a girl in Vassar, and a boy at Phillips Exeter Academy.

Born in Buffalo, Minnesota, Margaret Culkin Banning was
graduated from Vassar in 1912; received a certificate from the
Chicago School of Civics and Philanthropy in 1913; and was
married in 1914. During the World War she spent some time in
England and Holland. In Duluth, Minnesota, where she makes
her permanent home, Mrs. Banning is an ardent worker for community fund and crusade movements, and recently attended the
1934 Mobilization for Human Needs Conference at Washington.

Since 1920, Mrs. Banning has published one novel a year, and
contributed numerous essays and short stories to *Harper's*, the *Saturday Evening Post*, the *Delineator*, and other magazines—though
she often says she would rather read than write.

Mrs. Banning usually spends her winters in the South. She is
an enthusiastic equestrienne and plays excellent bridge.

Among her novels are *Country Club People*, *The Women of the
Family*, *The Town's Too Small*, and *The Third Son*.

∽ ∽

W E EXPECT so much. Out of our inadequacies, our frus-
trations, our hopes, and affections we adults build up
towers of demands on the young. I sometimes think the towers
are higher for girls than for boys. Every new achievement of
woman gives us a new ambition for the young girl and suggests
further preparation. We are continually adding to what we think
she should know, and hardly ever subtracting.

[1] Reprinted from *Harper's Magazine*, December, 1933. Used by permission of
Margaret Culkin Banning and Brandt and Brandt, author's agents.

I have a daughter who is seventeen years old. Thinking this over, I find that in the last six months I have expected her to know how to do these varied things:

Pass College Board examinations in chemistry, French, and Latin.

Decide on her preferences among further studies with a view to concentration of effort and ultimately to earning her own living.

Write a Latin poem.

Meet a great many strangers pleasantly.

Handle her own personal expenses on a small allowance and not ask me for additional money.

Play golf and tennis, one in the competition of tournaments.

Dance well.

Face the brutality of stag lines at parties.

Read intelligently such books as *The Imitation of Christ*, Emily Dickinson's *Poems*, Kay Boyle's *First Lover*, and William Faulkner's *Light in August*.

Order the food for simple but formal meals as well as provide plenty of provisions for the irregular hospitality of a country cottage and yet keep the marketing bills within a stipulated monthly amount.

Select several evening dresses, with the understanding that each must cost less than twenty dollars, and keep on hand the right kind of clothes for all her sports and activities.

Keep her clothes reasonably clean and unwrinkled.

Refrain from drinking without being a prig.

Prevent the boys who "took her out" from indulging in necking.

Write necessary letters of courtesy as well as the letter she wanted to write.

Leave the kitchen in order after impromptu entertaining at night, no matter how late it happens to be.

Be agreeable to her relatives and to those family friends in whom she has no interest.

Drive a car without accidents, wash it, and change a tire.

Swim.

Ride in a drag hunt.

Keep some of her day for herself.

It sounds as if I got my ideas of parenthood from Simon Legree. I am slightly ashamed of that list because there are so many things on it that I myself cannot do. Nor did she succeed in achieving the measure of perfection, as a crumpled fender, an irritated aunt, and various other things proved. But none the less that is what I expected of my daughter. These attainments and facilities and habits are ones which I want her to have. I do not want to cross anything off that list, and after a few moments' thought I shall probably find myself lengthening it.

I suppose too that it may seem confused and incoherent, if not pointless, this array of domestic and athletic and financial and social and intellectual accomplishments. Why must a girl know so much? Why do I want her equipped to face the strain of a modern ball room as well as to enter an office or classroom or laboratory? Why do I want her to clean a kitchen as well as write Latin verse?

The answer is that I believe that it is necessary. Her equipment must be diversified because I do not know what her future will be. Her future set-up is not so clear as that of a young man. It is beyond prophecy. Nor do I want her stultified or cramped by my notions of properly independent womanhood, for I suspect that the future independence of women will be more generous and more companionable than it was in its inception. A girl today should certainly be prepared to earn her own living but, at the same time, she should be prepared to manage her life successfully if someone else earns it for her. She may be a mother or a spinster, a scientist or a society woman, and she will want to do a good job in any case. Whether she works in an office or lives a life of amusement, she must be familiar with some forms of exercise. And as I believe that some domestic responsibility, feather weight or backbreaking, will ultimately become her personal problem, she should know how to handle that when it comes.

It is easy for a parent to be presumptuous in assuming the future of his child. I have two friends whose main business in life is bringing up their daughters. One is rich and a widower. One is a divorced woman who, successfully enough, earns her own living but is not wealthy. Their points of view are divergent and yet their ideals are so identical that they fascinate me. For both of these parents want their girls to be well educated, aristocratic in the bravest sense, competent, and happy. They chose the schools for the girls with the greatest care and, curiously enough, they chose the same schools. But outside of the schools they shape them absolutely differently. The woman so wants her daughters to be free from dependence on any man and so able to stand alone that she has almost isolated them among her own ideals. The man, who cannot conceive that his daughters will not marry, is insistent that they develop every grace. He promotes their social popularity. Both the man and the woman have said to me on separate occasions when I have brought the conversation to the point of considering a social upheaval, "Whatever happens, my girls would be adequate. They could meet any situation." But it is true that all four of the girls are at times self-conscious and unhappy. I have never seen girls suffer so much at a mixed house-party as that woman's daughters; and the man's daughters are completely at a loss if they fall into a company in which the conversation is so intellectual that it forgets certain graces and courtesies. If, by any chance, their lives should shape themselves differently from what their parents so firmly expect, these girls will doubtless always be self-conscious.

Until a girl's emotions reach fulfillment or are diverted into the pursuit of some major interest, her life is a gamble. This is far more true of girls than boys, and it is why I think a girl often needs to know things that exceed or even contradict a parent's ambition for her or a girl's ambition for herself.

From the essential things, one honestly tries to separate prejudices or favoritisms. For example, I do not think that every girl need know how to ride. Plenty of girls are afraid of horses and cannot overcome the fear; and plenty of them cannot afford the sport. Nor is Latin an essential knowledge. There are a few things on the list of accomplishments I wanted for my own daughter that are reflections of special aptitudes discovered in her or reflected desires of my own. But one can quickly weed them out, and essential things are still indicated.

Before going any farther one must take into account the vast diversity of education. How much can a girl learn under ordinary circumstances or under the best circumstances? What is offered in this country in the way of education and training to girls between twelve and twenty? It is a long range. There are those astonishing schools where a "good seat in the saddle" will almost insure a diploma; there are serious and gratifying boarding schools and convents; there are others that in their feeble and expensive way try to maintain class distinctions in the minds of young girls. Most inclusive of all there are the high schools. The possibilities for a girl's continuing education are divided among a number of women's colleges, some good church schools which are liberal as well as devout, and many universities.

Nearly every girl, even in the horsey schools, will be taught to read and write and cipher. In the best schools she will learn to study and become aware that the mind is a fine instrument for use and pleasure. She will be given information about Macbeth, Walter Pater, geometry, musical history, and other unallied subjects. If she goes to college, this knowledge will probably—not always, by any means—be importantly increased. In a girls' school or college she will also learn the problems and failures and satisfactions of utopias for women. In a high school or coeducational university she will, as a rule, learn enough facts to keep her there from year to year.

On the whole, I should say that most of what a girl learns in her classes at school will fade very quickly. The reading and writing, a trifle of geography, and a fragment of history will perhaps remain. She will remember names like Longfellow and Emerson. But little factual knowledge will stick to her mind if hers is the general girl's education, unless she goes on studying past the point at which most girls stop. I believe that a girl should know how to think, how to concentrate; and we have a right to expect that the academic side of her life, the schooling proper, will do this for her.

What I want to enumerate (and try to elucidate) are those other kinds of knowledge and additional skills which a girl should accumulate while her future is hanging in the balance. Like my own daughter, she may intend, as seriously as one can at seventeen, to study chemistry; but she may be deflected from that purpose when she begins to study economics or meets a man from Harvard. I do not want, because she has a special interest now, either to neglect it or let it color her life to such an extent that she will be unhappy or inadequate if her desires change and her habits of life turn out to be quite different from those which I imagine for her or those she dreams for herself. I want her to know the things that will stand her in good stead if she is poor; or if she is rich; if the state is communist or republican; if she is happily married, divorced, or remains single; if she should marry a man stationed in China or in an army post; if she builds herself a cottage in Carolina or has a job in a bank in New York.

I know only one way to approach the problem. It is true that I cannot foretell what her individual life will be, but I know what a woman's life in the world involves today and what obligations women as a sex have assumed for tomorrow. For those I can to some extent prepare her, because I can see into what divisions her duties must inevitably fall. She will have a business life of some sort, even if it is limited to paying her bills or shopping on credit. She will have a domestic life almost certainly, for domestic life persists even in strange new forms. She will have many social dealings with men and women. She will have personal relations with herself. For these four things I want, by hook or crook, by play or work, to fit her, and when I say "her" now, I do not mean only my own daughter but the daughters of my friends and of strangers and the multitudes of girls in schools and behind counters. All of these four things they must face. Into these four channels of life we must direct a girl's knowledge and her skill.

§

When I say business dealings I do not mean a job. I think a girl should know how to earn her living, of course. She can no longer count on an income from any other source. When I think of all the women who thought five years ago that they were "fixed for life" and are now in a desperate way, trying to sell lingerie or cosmetics, I hardly think this point need be disputed. For everyone knows as many of these unfortunate and usually unskilled women as I do. A girl who cannot earn her living may be arrogantly set apart by her unearned income (and that, as I say, is terribly precarious today), but she is usually an adventurer, living by her wits and the practice of her emotions or by setting up claims to devotion. I do not care how happily married she may be; she would be even more happily married if she knew that she could earn her living.

Often it isn't necessary for her to do it, at least continually. But any girl I bring up is going to know the delightful feeling of an earned dollar. The sense of earning, the personal confidence it gives a girl, the awareness that her energy or ability has a market value is immeasurably valuable. That knowledge keeps a girl from all sorts of secret discontents and fears. If she marries it is apt to make her relations with her husband truer and freer, because, while she may quite properly be living on his income, she is not in terror lest he lose it or tire of her. The ability of a woman to earn money has made some difficult married situations, no doubt, but it has destroyed so much hypocrisy and humiliation that there is no question that it is one of the most important things a girl should know. Also, a girl should know how to earn money so that she may realize the value of a dollar either given or spent. Very extravagant and very stingy women are usually those who do not know how to earn a nickel.

When my daughter finishes her schooling she will, I think, have found a way to earn her living. But if she has not—and it is not discreditable for a girl to be undirected professionally even at twenty-one or -two—I shall send her to a business college for a few months and then expect her to find a job. Any job, just as a boy would have to do. I would not let her stumble about, among parties and households, until she is thirty and then discover that her education had gone stale and that she had no method of earning except badgering her friends to buy trinkets or luxuries because of friendship.

Yet to be fair, it must be admitted that it is not always possible for every girl to know how to earn money. She may marry very young, sometimes advisedly. But even then she will have business dealings with the world. She will shop. She will market. She will be responsible for spending money. And this responsibility should be handled adequately. That is why when my daughter, on the twenty-eighth of July, has thirteen cents and no gasoline in her Ford, she has to get along as best she can until the first of August, afoot. That is why I let her do the marketing and give her only a certain amount to spend. That is why she is told that she can have a new evening dress if she can find one for less than twenty dollars.

The world has been full to the brim with charming, dishonest women who have had a whole lot to do with steering it on the rocks. They can be just as charming if they are honest, and that they cheat is not exclusively their fault, for husbands, fathers, and shopkeepers have winked in an amused or surly way at the notion that women always spend more than they should and, in some twisted way, have linked this failing up to a tribute to man's guardianship and superiority.

That is very tiresome. It is also old stuff. A girl should know how to write a check—and when I say check I include an entry on a check stub. The ciphering in public schools often helps us out on this point by including in common arithmetic the writing of checks. A girl should know that a bank account is not a bottomless pit. But if she has no bank account she can at least know how much cash or what portion of her parents' or husband's credit she can spend.

She should know, and at a reasonably early age, something about insurance and investments. This does not have to be expert knowledge but it should be a knowledge definitely and closely related to her income and responsibilities. I know young teachers who almost pride themselves on "never having a cent." For some reason they consider it spirited. But it shows that, in spite of being educators themselves, they lack one of the forms of knowledge every girl should have—that of proper business dealings with the world.

It gets down to this: a girl should know how to handle what money she has, whether it is five dollars or a half million. The sight of a girl who is putting herself through school by waiting on table gives me a complete confidence as to that girl's ability to keep out of bankruptcy all her life. But the girl who says, "I couldn't possibly afford it! But it was so adorable that I just had to have it," has not been taught how to spend. And she will be saying the same thing all the rest of her life unless a new social order chokes the words in her throat.

§

It seems to me beyond question that a girl should know something about domestic life and household management. Here I run wild with preferences. For I would rather have a girl know how to clean a sink (or a bathtub) than make a lemon pie. I prefer knowledge of cleanliness to knowledge of cookery, and accomplishment in neatness to fine sewing.

I myself think cooking is one of the most satisfactory things in the world because it is so tangible an accomplishment. But though we make hundreds of glasses of jelly in my own house every summer, I have not thought it necessary for my daughter to know how to make jelly.

I have insisted that she know how many pounds of peas to buy for six people and at what season to buy melons and avoid grapes, as well as the difference between shoulder, rib, and loin lamb chops, and a standing or rolled roast of beef. I want her to know how to make good coffee, good tea, broil a chop or a steak, make a salad, and put a meal on the table without getting breathless. I want her to know how to get breakfast. Beyond that I would leave further knowledge about cookery to the pressure and temptation of her future circumstances. Who knows what cookery will be necessary in the future?

I believe that a girl should know how to take a temperature and care for a minor illness or accident. She should know how to make a bed. Few do. I think she should know that there is no peace of mind in a confused or disorderly room. She should know how to arrange flowers and make something charming out of six miserable calendulas if necessary. But, lest you imagine that I think her household talents should be administrative or decorative only, let me add at once that she should know how to wash clothes and press clothes, if not iron to a fine finish. This is for the reason that if she is confronted with poverty it would be more easy to slip into habits of uncleanliness than actually to starve. But I do not think she needs to know how to make darning look like fine tapestry.

These things are all relevant to my own conviction that a household's grace and much of its happiness are dependent on order and cleanliness and beauty. Even if a girl lives in a cabin on a boat or in a service flat many of these aptitudes will be useful. If she has a normal household they will be basic.

There is one other thing about domestic life that it is necessary for a girl to know, and that is how to get along well with her family. In every family the effort at harmony must start somewhere, and men and boys succumb more easily to business moods or bad golf scores or boils. A girl should know how to appear cheerful when she is not cheerful and look serene at the table when she is troubled. It is part of her woman's job.

One always feels, at intervals, that girls should know more about the care of infants and children than most of them do. Yet it has always seemed to me that any artificial attempt to stimulate a love of babies in young girls was bound to fail. It is one of the things which we can leave to nature, and heaven knows that we are doing so much of nature's work for her now that she ought to be willing to keep on at that one job. The most ignorant or most frivolous girl, when she is brought up against the problems of motherhood and must take on the care of a child, learns with marvelous quickness and retention—if she wants to. Every fine quality in a girl pours into her first experience in motherhood. It seems to me if a girl knows that a household is normally made up of people of different ages, if she is affectionate with her grandparents and pleasant to a three-year-old visiting niece, that she has the fundamental idea.

Domestic life weaves into social life, and sometimes the fabrics blend. But social relations, especially those with boys and men, are so important that a girl should have special knowledge about them to guide her. I make no exceptions. Every young girl is involved. She may escape business dealings almost entirely; she may touch domestic life only with the tips of her fingers; but she is sure to have social relations that will bring her pain and happiness. And while she is a girl she will give a major part of her imaginings, her hopes, and her intentions to the relations between herself and men, no matter how she is brought up.

Some parents and guardians scorn such absorption and treat it as if it were of no account, or a little comical. And there is an academic school of thought which considers it as an old-fashioned preoccupation sloughed off entirely by the modern girl. This is not true. The normal modern girl, without abandoning the victories of feminism, and accepting its responsibilities, does not even want to imagine a life in which men play no part. Therefore, she should be fortified by accomplishment and equipment for such relations.

One begins with those general social relations which lead to closer ones between individuals, and for these a knowledge of how to dress, how to play games, how to dance, how to talk well, and conduct oneself in company are the major points. It is very necessary for a girl to know how to wear her clothes to advantage and make the most of herself physically. This includes what I call, rather stumblingly, a discovery of her own personality as expressed by her appearance. When a girl is sure of that she will go on to learn such minor things as whether to use a dark shade of powder or to wear a white bathing suit. She should know that it is not necessary to be beautiful in order to be charming. She should know that no well-dressed person thinks about her looks all the time.

She must know how to use her voice. The shrill clatter of some girls' voices definitely destroys their charm. I do not mean to suggest affectation or the grafting of accents which are unsuitable and out of place. But a girl should speak so that it is pleasant to listen to her. If this were universally true fewer homes would break up. If a girl is surrounded by people with raucous voices she can always go to the talkies and listen to one of the few actresses who speak beautifully, and learn from them how musical the English language can be.

She should know how to dance. Dancing is essential to a girl's social confidence and it is the great leveller. There are dances for five cents a whirl and dances to which only several thousand dollars a season will give admittance, but at all of them are the same competitions and sufferings and successes. Uncounted parents have tried to find a solution for the cruelty of the modern dances but there does not seem to be any except that a girl should know how to dance very well. Otherwise a girl should not be exposed to a ball where mercy is left in the cloakrooms. She herself should know, if her parents do not, that it is better to stay at home than to be pilloried.

But dancing is not enough. A girl must know other sports. She should swim. This, like dancing, is within the reach of every purse, for we have public beaches as well as public dance halls. She should know how to swim both for safety and for pleasure. But after reaching this point I should let a girl choose her other sports. In my own family we have been pretty catholic and had even our archery and fencing attempts—these at camp and school. They petered out and left the more conventional, widely shared sports.

A girl who knows how to drive a golf ball a decent distance or return a serve well in tennis, or ride a horse without wondering if he is going to throw her, has a resource, a means of healthy development, and an opportunity to meet men in their sports. I think a girl should know how to do one such thing quite well. If it is golf, let it be golf. If it is riding, let it be that. But to know one sport to a high point of excellence seems to me far better than to have a smattering of all of them. This applies particularly to one indoor sport, bridge. I am not at all sure that girls should be allowed to play bridge at all unless they really know the game. This country is too crowded with women who sort cards and can do little else except tell one suit from another and make mistakes, whose minds are cluttered by rules that they can't follow. I do not care personally whether a girl ever touches a card or not. But if she plays bridge I think she should know the game.

I feel strongly about drinking. I know of no valid reason why a girl should know how to drink. It will do her no physical good. It will steadily decrease her ability to have a good time without a drink. She should know how not to drink without making a fuss about it or calling attention to herself.

But these are strange times and unsteady ones. This is not the age of drawing the skirt aside. It is the age of tolerance. It is suitable here to mention also that a girl should know how to control gossip and protect a friend's good name. She should know how to be amusing but to avoid coarseness.

I forgot to mention that a girl should know how to drive a car. Often a modern girl has to know how to drive a car for safety alone. Also it adds to her general competence. She should be able to handle any make of car, know how to drive without showing off or posing in the middle of traffic. I said in the beginning that I wanted my daughter to know how to wash a car and change a tire. That is partly in the interests of economy and partly because those things cement the affection of ownership.

But there are other things she must know in addition to all these. For men are going to disappoint her, sometimes at the best, always at the worst. Jobs and work can go terribly stale. Her domestic life is bound to be interrupted and terrified by illness and calamity sooner or later. Is she to have no preparation against such things?

I think she should have it and can have it. In the first place, she should know how to read. I mean that she should know how to transfer the contents of a printed page to her mind, not just skim over a few columns of movie gossip. She should be able to get something to rest and stimulate her out of imaginative literature and critical literature. If possible, she should know how to play the piano; for if you are in trouble your radio will drive you mad but your piano will be your comfort.

She must know how to be alone. Much of an average woman's life has lonely stretches in it, which will frighten her if she has not learned as a girl the pleasure of being alone. If she has to run to a woman's club or to the telephone to keep herself from solitude, she lacks proper resource. She does not really destroy or use her solitude. So I think a girl should be taught that it is a pleasure to be alone, to have time for a solitary walk, for thought and for figuring out what every human being has to do before he is through, why he exists at all.

If I am demanding, it is because I care so much. I know what a great burden is on the girl of today; and for all her apparent nonchalance, she knows it too. She must carry all the new responsibilities we can conjure up for her, earn her living, and somehow restore and improve much of the charm that harsher feminists tossed aside. She must be able to earn her way, pay her own fare, mark her own ballot, and yet have every quality of feminine companionship. She must meet the terrible competition of emotion in the world today; which is worse than it ever was because of the early start it gets and the prolongation that both men and women now insist upon.

If we had a safe, settled adult world to open to a girl, if we could promise her even a choice between a small job and a good man's love, it would be different. But we are so confused ourselves that we cannot distinguish between the basic and the temporary. We know only this: that few of the dangers girls ever faced have been destroyed and new ones have been added. Sometimes it seems to me that a girl today has to know all that any woman ever had to know, except making soap and candles and spinning yarn. And I think she could do those things if they were necessary.

I knew I should find myself adding to that list. For there is another thing I must not forget. She should know, no matter if she is cheated, no matter if she is thwarted, that quarreling with men is self-destructive.

Of Ships and Travel

Alice and the *Aquitania* [1]

CHRISTOPHER MORLEY

Christopher Morley is probably the most popular essayist in America. With his first published collection of sketches he won a large reading public who have followed his subsequent books with undiminished relish. His skill is not confined to the gentle art of essay-writing, but extends to many other literary forms. He has written novels and poems, edited magazines, produced plays, and for years has conducted his own column, "The Bowling Green," now a weekly feature of the *Saturday Review of Literature*.

The son of English parents, Christopher Morley was born in 1890, in Haverford, Pennsylvania. His father was at that time professor of mathematics at Haverford College. From that institution Morley was graduated at the age of twenty. On a Rhodes Scholarship he went to New College at Oxford, and spent three years in study and continental travel.

Returning to the United States, he worked for the publishing house of Doubleday, Page and Company. After four years at that job he became an editor of the *Ladies' Home Journal*—"one of the willful men who edit a ladies' journal," he says of himself. Next he joined the Philadelphia *Evening Ledger* as a columnist, and here, "in a rolltop desk," was born the "Old Mandarin," whose enigmatic philosophies in free verse compose the delightful pages of Morley's *Translations from the Chinese*. In 1920, Mr. Morley joined the New York *Evening Post*, to conduct "The Bowling Green," which department he took with him when he became associate editor of the *Saturday Review*.

In private life Mr. Morley is a commuter. Like thousands of others, he journeys daily from the North Shore of Long Island to New York City. He writes of life as he lives it, skillfully blending good reporting with keen observation and gentle humor.

The best of his essays have been collected into one volume published by Doubleday, Doran and Company, entitled *Essays by Christopher Morley*. His novels include *Where the Blue Begins, Parnassus on Wheels, Thunder on the Left*.

[1] From the *Saturday Review of Literature*. Reprinted by permission of Christopher Morley.

SHIPPING business is bad; it is grievous to see so many good vessels laid up in the Erie Basin and in the alcoves of the Gowanus Canal. But *Alice M. Moran*, "of 29 net tons measurement," says her certificate, still puts in a lively twelve-hour day.

We were talking to Buck McNeil at the Battery Pier. If you have ever fallen—or jumped—overboard from the Battery seawall, you know Buck. He is the fellow who pulled you out. In his 26 years as boatman at that pier he has rescued 290 people. At least he has been credited with 290; the number is really more than that, for Buck has a habit of walking away when he has got the pessimist ashore. He keeps in his pocket the certificate of the U. S. Life Saving Medal of Honor, "for acts of Unusual Heroism," and on his watch-chain is the gold medal of the Dock Department, given him by Mayor Hylan. But in spite of hard times, people don't seem to go off the deep end so much nowadays. Buck hasn't had to go into the harbor for anyone in the last two years. He's just as pleased, for he says there are occasional twinges of rheumatism. We wanted to ask Buck whether the Carnegie Medal committee knew about all this, but just then *Alice M. Moran* came steaming across from Jersey City with a bone in her teeth. This was the Club's first chance in many years to go tugboating, and we hastened aboard.

We are not the first to raise a small chantey of praise in honor of *Alice*, for her skipper, Anton Huseby, proudly showed us an admirable article written about her by Roy Crandall in *Gas Logic* of last September. No one could improve on Mr. Crandall's excellent story, which Captain Huseby keeps in the pilot house, and which includes also a lifelike photograph of *Alice's* snug galley with the skipper, and Mr. Banks, the mate, and Mr. Anderson, the chief, and I think also Selverson, the rope-artist on deck, sitting down to chow, with Bill Paton, the Scotch cook, in the background. The deck hand is the lad who can toss a four-inch hawser so that it loops itself right round the big iron cleat when *Alice* comes alongside a pier. And Bill Paton is still a leal Scot though he admits it's a long time since he tasted haggis. We apologize to Bill for having thought he said he came from Canarsie. It wasn't Canarsie but Carnoustie, which is near Dundee. This record of the Three Hours for Lunch Club's visit doesn't attempt to compete with Mr. Crandall's narrative. But all days on a tugboat are different, and this one happened to be our own.

We were remembering that it was just forty-five years ago this month that the Lords of Committee of Privy Council for Trade granted to a certain Conrad Korzeniowski his "Certificate of Competency as Master." For that reason I was the more interested in Captain Huseby's own license. It reads that he "can safely be entrusted with the duties and responsibilities of master of freight and towing steam vessels of any gross tons upon the waters of bays, sounds, and rivers and to Dumping Grounds off Scotland Light, and Pilot of any Steamer of any tonnage upon New York Bay and Harbor to Yonkers, Staten Island Sound, South Amboy, Newark Bay, and tributaries of the East River to Stepping Stones." The commander of a tug is a more important navigator than a lubber perhaps realizes. He is a seaman to his finger-tips, and performs dexterities of maneuver that astound any lover of craft. And when he takes a steamship in or out of dock he climbs to the big fellow's bridge and takes charge up there. Even if she's as big as the *Aquitania*, it's the tugboat captain who is up aloft giving the word to his leash of soft-nosed whelps, nuzzling like beagles under her tall side.

Alice had already done a good five hours' work when we boarded her. She left her berth in Brooklyn at 6 A.M. First she went to Pier 57 North River and brought the *Jacques Cartier* to Pier 3, Army Base. Then she docked the steamer *Tergestea*, and the transport *St. Mihiel* just in from Honolulu. Then she took the barge *Dwyer* 17 across to Pier 7, Central Railroad of New Jersey. It was there, I suppose, that she got the surprising news from her home office that four members of the Club had received permission to come aboard. In older days the owners of tugboat fleets sometimes signaled their captains by intricate codes of waving from the office windows in Battery Place. Perhaps there still is an emergency signal that means Visitors for Lunch.

We were hardly in the roomy pilot house before sturdy *Alice* was again about her affairs. The first thing one noticed was that tugboats, by old tradition, steer backward: unlike social craft the wheel preserves the old theory of the tiller. When the wheel is turned to starboard, the tugboat turns to port. So the ordinary merchant seaman or yachtsman is a dangerous fellow at a tugboat helm until he has learned this difference by instinct.

We went down past Governor's Island, which seemed empty and peaceful. A solitary officer was riding on a horse beside the big polo field. Captain Huseby recalled with some amusement a thing that happened (but not to his own clients), a few years ago. A big cattle-barge for the Union Stock Yards was rounding the Battery when someone hit her amidships, "right in the belly." She began to founder and the nearest safety was the army pier at Governor's Island. She was got alongside just in time and drove off several hundred terrified steers and sheep who fled in panic among barracks and parade grounds, putting major generals and polo players to flight. That day Governor's Island's dignity was badly shaken. It must have looked like a Wild West show. We had always wondered at the origin of the name Buttermilk Channel for the strait between Governor's Island and Brooklyn. Did it imply that mariners of softer temper kept in that sheltered reach while men of strong gizzard plowed up the main slot? No; Captain Huseby thinks it was named when the Brooklyn shore was all farmland and there was a rustic refreshment stand for thirsty boatmen near where the Hamilton Avenue ferry is now.

At Erie Basin and along the Gowanus Inlet one observes the curious transition in the naming of ships. There we saw old-timers like the *Buccaneer*, romantic names like *Silver Sandal*, *Western Ocean*, *Munamar*, alongside the *Commercial Guide*, the *Bird City*, the *Commercial Trader*, the *Cities Service Empire*. The *Eastern Temple* is a sulphur trader from Louisiana. The *Gibraltar* of Glasgow, a sturdy British tramp with salmon and black funnel, showed an active riffle of steam from her escape. The *West Isleta* was canted far over to starboard so we supposed she was loading. Among many idle bottoms it was encouraging to see these signs of activity. The *Cities Service Empire* was evidently very much on the job, but some of her neighbors lay rusting and forlorn. What a setting for a mystery story, one of these grim idle freighters.

We lay off Owl's Head, an old mansion on the hill at Bay Ridge, waiting for the *Alaskan*. Two old wooden hulks are on the beach there, surely a disgrace to the pride of New York Harbor. They have been there many years, and boatmen are sensitive about these things. Why doesn't the Port Authority destroy them?

In the sunny noon, which seemed more like April than November, we tarried for our client. The great heights of Manhattan showed faintly through soft haze. Along that Brooklyn shore one is aware of the enormous auxiliaries of power and service that lie behind the tall frontages of the office world. The Bush piers, the Edison plant, the Long Island Railroad freight terminal give one plenty to think about. The incredibly vast warehouses of the Army Base add a vibration of anxiety. Then the *Alaskan* of the American-Hawaiian Line came striding up the Narrows, in light from Boston. We had thought she might be the original *Alaskan*, whom F. R. had met years ago in the Straits of Magellan. But she must be a younger vessel, and her bow showed traces of a previous name, *Wheaton*. It was fine to see *Alice* slide alongside of her, running parallel and at exactly the same speed, and gently edge in with hardly a creak from the log fenders. Bill Banks took the wheel, Captain Huseby ran up the tall green ladder *Alice* carries at her side. With unbelievable address she was swung and pushed to her berth. Her neighbor there was a well-known Bermudian friend, the *Fort St. George*. Not far away were the handsome *Eastern Prince* and *Japanese Prince* with their emblems of the Prince of Wales's three feathers. Just above was the pier of the Brazilian Lloyd, and a very handsome ship, the *Niel Maersk* of Svendborg. A few hours round the waterfront make geography very real.

Now it was time for lunch. Tugboat meals are a noble tradition, and Bill Paton, even though four guests had been put upon him unexpectedly, was ready for the test. No one ever tasted better corned beef and cabbage, boiled potatoes, spinach, coffee with condensed milk. The bowl of apples had been polished until they glittered. Bill's doughnuts, little balls of crisp fluff, compare to the average doughnut of commerce as Bacon's essays to a newspaper editorial. When we asked him if he ever gave his crew a Scotch haggis he replied that there was hardly enough room to compound one in that galley, where the stove warms the backs of the eaters as they sit. But I think he could do it if it were laid upon him. His eyes shone as we recalled how Captain Bone has the haggis played in with pipers aboard the *Transylvania*, and the cook is honored for his art with a tumbler of neat Highland elixir. The next time *Transylvania* comes up the harbor I think if Bill Paton happens to see her he will look out from his galley, see her commander high aloft in gold stripes and yellow gloves, and say to himself "Yon's the skipper wha kens aboot a haggis."

What's our next job? we asked, already feeling that for one day *Alice's* affairs were our concern. We were to take out the *Ashburton* of London, said Captain Huseby. We had noticed her at Pier 2, flying her Blue Peter, and her house-flag, with the emblem of a swan. "The Hungry Goose they call it in the old country," said Bill Paton.

But the *Ashburton* wasn't quite ready for us yet, so we tied up and lay comfortably in a warm drowse. Gray gulls were squealing, New York shone faintly through a yellow veil of sun. The radio in the pilot house was turned on, and through peaceful siesta some humorist from Newark was singing hunting songs about view hallos and gentry in scarlet "galloping, galloping, galloping." We ourselves felt more like snoring, snoring, snoring. Another member of the *Moran* family, *Eugene F.*, sidled in and lay alongside us with calm brotherly affection. One member sat on the stringpiece of the pier, sketching the pair. Others walked along beneath *Ashburton's* comely stern, watched the last of her cargo going aboard, learned from her mate that she was bound for Newport News and then Australia. A Diesel barge called *Corning* went buzzing fussily in and out of various piers, carrying only one huge case which looked like a crated automobile. It was like a small dog with a bone he hasn't decided where to bury. *Corning* barked

every now and then with a loud and very unshiplike-sounding
horn. From *Alice's* pilot house we heard the radio cry "This
quaint minuet is redo*l*ent with the atmosphere of bygone days."

Then suddenly there was a hail from *Ashburton's* stern. We woke
from our drowse on the pierhead. *Alice* and *Eugene F.* sprang to life.
One of the Club's own members, master mariner himself, cast off
Ashburton's stern lines from the big iron cleat. Water boiled under
her counter. We took her out and swung her toward open sea,
feeling we had done well. But our greatest adventure was still to
come.

We came up harbor again in the pink light of late afternoon,
too wise even to try to match words against that cluster of sta-
lagmites that will never be described by deliberate intention;
only, if ever, by accident. Perhaps James Bone came as near it
*as anyone: "The City of Dreadful Height." It is a much steeper
view from the deck of a tug than from the high terraces of a liner.
We steered for the deep notch of Broadway, as the big ships do,
and rounded the bend of the island. F. A. remembered that the
last time we had come up the bay in a tug was the night President
Harding died, when some great building in Battery Place had left
its lights burning toward sea in the pattern of a huge cross. "I'm
afraid they wouldn't do it again for poor old Harding," was someone's comment. Yet no man need be grudged whatever light he
can get as he heads down those dark Narrows.

We passed the *American Farmer* at her pier: a merchantman of
letters in spite of her bucolic name. The other day she brought
over from London the new edition of Sir Thomas Browne; and is
it not her commander, good Captain Myddleton, who told us
long ago that he always keeps the General Catalogue of the Oxford University Press in the chart-room, for momentary relief during hours of fog or soundings? But our minds were on other matters. The *Aquitania* was now at Quarantine and would be up
shortly—a full day late, after a bad voyage. *Alice* was to help
dock her.

At Pier 42 is a little rendezvous where the *Moran* family and
their friends the *Barretts* wait for the prima donnas to come in.

We tarried there in a plain, undemonstrative family group. From the various errands of the day these stout work-women of the harbor came puffing in. They seemed to wipe their hands on their aprons and sit rocking gently on beamy bottoms to talk things over before the big job. They filled water coolers, the men took a sluice at the fresh-water hose. There was *Joseph H. Moran*, bigger than ourself; and *Helen B. Moran* with a small white dog on board, very alert and eager of eye, much aware of his responsibility as the only dog among so many informal human beings. He stood up with front paws rigid against *Helen B.'s* bulwarks and watched the other kinsmen arrive with critical attention. Oliver (who notices everything) says the small white dog was furiously annoyed when in the middle of his supervisions one of the men sprayed him humorously with a mouthful of drinking water. Certainly it was a liberty, and the more so if it was done by someone on the *Howard C. Moore* or the *Downer X*, who were not *Morans* or *Barretts*. But I did not see this myself, for at that moment F. R. was telling me of his excitement in reading Defoe's *Journal of the Plague Year* and asking me (so it seemed to my morbid mind) why none of us could write as well as Defoe.

We lay in a knot, haunch to haunch, at the end of Pier 42. *Eugene F. Moran* had followed us faithfully from Brooklyn. *Grace Barrett* was there, and *Richard J. Barrett*, and *R. J. Barrett*. It must be fun to have a big family and a tugboat to name after each of them. *John Nichols*, however, kept a little in the offing. He was too proud to join our little gab, for it is *John Nichols's* captain who goes aboard the big liner and commands the whole fleet of tugs. The rest of us sociabled our soft noses together, our upward poking bows muzzled with the big fenders that look like a brown bear climbing aboard. Above the soft aroma of the North River was a good smell of cooking. We lay in an eddy of it, for all galleys were busy.

Aquitania loomed up in the haze. Only someone very important could arrive so quietly, so steadily, so sure of herself. We had the oblique profile of her, best for both women and ships. Every slant of her seemed to accept homage. She took it as her due, yet not wholly unconscious of it, for she was still a little sore from discourtesies outside. At sea, alone with gray trigonometry, she is only a little thing. Here she was queen. In that soft light she did not come, she grew. But these were the thoughts of lubbers. The urchin tugs (I am sorry to switch metaphors so often) have no time for awe. They swarm about her skirts and hustle her with sooty grasp.

Our little fleet throbbed into action. It was like letting a pack of well-trained beagles out of a kennel. No one needed to be told anything. The routine has been perfected in every detail. *John Nichols* turned downstream to meet her. *Joseph H.* and *Helen B.* shot up ahead of us with a scurry of froth. *Grace Barrett*, pirouetting on her solid heel, twirled across our bow and took the inside track along the pierheads. Behind this interference *Eugene* and ourself and *Howard Moore* followed upstream. There was a very strong ebb, Captain Huseby had told us. But there was no difficulty of wind, a gentle breeze from S.W. It was pink November dusk at its mildest.

Alice and *Eugene* went outward to join her. She came huge above us, steadily increasing. Now we had no eyes to note the movements of the other tugs, only to study this monstrous nobility of a ship. It must have been a bad voyage, for she looked dingy, rusted, and salted from water-line to funnels. High on her sloping stacks were crusts of salt. Her white-work was stained, her boot-topping green with scum. The safety nettings were still stretched along her steerage decks; even high on the promenade we could see them brailed up. Passengers at her rails looked down incuriously as we dropped astern. Just one more landing, they supposed.

We passed the notice board—*Propeller 8 feet beneath surface, Keep Clear*—and with *Eugene* slid in under her magnificent stern. Her bronze fans, turning unseen, slipped her cleanly along; we nosed busily into the very broth of her wake. Almost beneath the overhang we followed, dipping in the great swelling bubbles of her shove. It was like carrying the train of an empress. AQUITANIA, LIVERPOOL! Only the sharks have followed her closer than that. She was drawing 33½ feet at the rudder-post. The smooth taper of her hull, swimming forward ahead of us, made her seem suddenly fishlike. Beneath that skin of metal you could divine the intricate veinings and glands of her life: silvery shafts turning in a perspiration of oil, hot bulbs of light, white honeycombs of corridor, cell-like staterooms suddenly vacated. All the cunning structure of vivid life, and yet like everything living, so pitifully frail. Then Bill Banks the mate went forward with a boathook. He stood under her colossal tail with his rod poised like a lance. "My God," said Oliver, "he's going to harpoon her." We looked at *Eugene F.* and there, too, stood one with boathook pointed. Like two whaleboats we followed *Moby Dick*.

She swam steadily. A uniformed officer and two sailors looked down at us from the taffrail far above. There was superiority in that look. But *Alice M.* takes condescension from none. "Give us your rope," she cried. They said nothing. We continued to follow. A breath of anxiety seemed to pass over Captain Huseby and Bill Banks. For now we were almost abreast of the pier. Perhaps that ebb tide was on their minds. To deal with that ebb was our affair. They repeated the invitation. "Wait till we get word from the bridge," replied the officer calmly. The devil with the bridge, we could see *Alice* thinking. Her job is to get hold of a line and the sooner the better. At last it came, snaking downward. Bill Banks caught it, partly on the boathook and partly on his neck. The big hawser drooped after it, five inches thick of new rope. There was fierce haste to get it looped on the towing bitts astern. It was *Alice* who took *Aquitania's* first line, from the port quarter. "You've got to be careful taking a rope under way like this," said Captain Huseby spinning his wheel. "These big ships have a powerful suction."

Eugene F. took the second line. The next thing we realized a quick hitch-up had taken place, and we were towing in tandem. *R. J. Barrett* was coupled ahead of *Alice*, *Richard Barrett* was in line with *Eugene*. The quartet headed diagonally upstream. The big hawsers came taut and creaked. *Alice* trembled. Up at *Aquitania's* port bow were three other tugs pushing downward, side by side. Seven of us altogether on the port side. There must have been half a dozen to starboard, but what was happening there we couldn't see.

Alice shook with life. The churn from *R. J. Barrett* boiled past us. The mass of *Aquitania's* stern plus the flow of the whole Hudson watershed hung on a few inches of splice hooked over the bitts. The big ship stood unmoved as a cliff, while our quartet strained and quivered. *Morans* and *Barretts* dug their twirly heels into the slippery river and grunted with work. Steam panted with hot enjoyment. *Aquitania* didn't seem to care. She wasn't even looking at us. Her port side was almost deserted. Passengers were all to starboard looking for someone to say hello to. Lights began to shine from the ports. One was blocked with a wooden dead-light, proof of smashing weather. A single steward looked out calmly from the glory hole. It was all old business to him. For several minutes nothing seemed to happen. In midstream a big Socony tanker, almost loaded under with weight of oil, stood by to bring in fuel as soon as she was docked. John D. ready for business, we thought. There was no time to lose: she must sail again only 31 hours later. And in this, the very stress of the battle, they asked us, "How about some supper?" *Alice* had hold now. Apparently she could do practically all the rest of it herself. Captain Huseby was surprised when we said we were too excited to eat.

Gradually the big hull swung. The downward sweep of the tide crisped in a smacking surf against her side as she straightened out across the river. Her great profile brightened with lights in the thickening dusk. Now she was straight onto the opening of the pier. She blew once, very short, a deep, mellow rumble. Thanks! We all answered in chorus, with equal brevity. Sure! Our quartet slackened the pull, wheeled off at wider angles to safeguard her stern as she warped in. She had pivoted round the corner and was slowly easing against the camels, those floating rafts that keep her from rubbing. Captain Huseby now did his steering from the wheel at *Alice's* stern. The rest were at supper.

It was blue dark, 5:10 P.M. New Jersey had vanished except

for the bright words LIPTON'S TEA. *Aquitania's* stern was flush with the outer end of the pier. Her ensign came down. We could hardly believe it was all over.

Bill Paton was a little disappointed we could not stay for supper. But we had seen too much—and eaten too much lunch—to be hungry yet. "Next time let us know a day ahead," he remarked, "and we can really give you a meal." We tried to compliment the deck hand on his sure skill with a hawser. He was embarrassed. "I'm glad you were pleased," was his modest reply. They put us ashore at the end of the pier.

Why do people build or buy big steam yachts, we wondered. Surely a tugboat is the perfect craft. They build them on the Great Lakes—Green Bay, I think they said, was where *Alice* came from. You can get one like her for something like $100,000. A maiden voyage in a tugboat from Green Bay to New York would be a good trip to take.

Aquitania lay there, a blaze of lights, stewards busy carrying off baggage. *Alice* backed off with a curtseying motion, and vanished into the dark. She sleeps in Brooklyn.

Emblems of Hope

JOSEPH CONRAD

Josef Konrad (Korzeniowski) was born at Berdiczew in Russian Poland on December 3, 1857. His parents were Polish landowners whose family estates had diminished to some extent during the Napoleonic wars half a century earlier. Josef was but five years of age when his father was sent into exile for having participated in a series of secret meetings prior to an insurrection in Warsaw. Wife and son accompanied the exile into a number of Russian prison camps, but after suffering innumerable privations during the following three years Josef's mother passed away. Josef and his father returned to Poland shortly afterwards, but the lad was left an orphan when his father died five years later. Although his uncle gave him a comfortable home, a deep-seated love of the sea soon found expression in his removal to Marseilles in 1874. After making several short voyages during the following four years, he arrived in England in 1878 with hardly any command of English and still less inspiration to write. However he soon mastered the language and a few years later began to write *Almayer's Folly,*—anecdotes of people whom he had met earlier on the East coast of Borneo. This task occupied four or five years, but the finished work was a masterpiece of achievement for a newcomer to the language.

In 1894 he left the sea and made writing his profession, which he continued until his death in 1924. His foreign upbringing on the one hand and his varied personal experiences on the other place his works among the unparalleled "feats" of literature both in individual achievement and in accuracy of treatment. Among his best-known works might be listed *Youth, Typhoon, The Mirror of the Sea* and *The Nigger of the Narcissus.*

"The truth of the matter," writes Conrad, "is that my faculty to write in English is as natural as any other aptitude with which I might have been born. I have a strange and overpowering feeling that it had always been an inherent part of myself. English was for me neither a matter of choice nor adoption. The merest idea of choice had never entered my head. As to adoption—well, yes, there was adoption; but it was I who was adopted by the genius of the language which, directly I came out of the stammering stage, made me its own so completely that its very idioms I truly believe had a direct action on my temperament and fashioned my still plastic career."

ᖇᖙ   ᖇᖙ

I

B EFORE an anchor can ever be raised, it must be let go; and this perfectly obvious truism brings me at once to the subject of the degradation of the sea language in the daily press of this country.

Your journalist, whether he takes charge of a ship or a fleet, almost invariably "casts" his anchor. Now, an anchor is never cast, and to take a liberty with technical language is a crime against the clearness, precision, and beauty of perfected speech.

An anchor is a forged piece of iron, admirably adapted to its end, and technical language is an instrument wrought into perfection by ages of experience, a flawless thing for its purpose. An anchor of yesterday (because nowadays there are contrivances like mushrooms and things like claws, of no particular expression or shape — just hooks) — an anchor of yesterday was in its way a most efficient instrument. To its perfection its size bears witness, for there is no other appliance so small for the great work it has to do. Look at the anchors hanging from the cat-heads of a big ship! How tiny they are in proportion to the great size of the hull! Were they made of gold they would look like trinkets, like ornamental toys, no bigger in proportion than a jewelled drop in a woman's ear. And yet upon them will depend, more than once, the very life of the ship.

An anchor is forged and fashioned for faithfulness; give it ground that it can bite, and it will hold till the cable parts, and then, whatever may afterwards befall its ship, that anchor is "lost." The honest, rough piece of iron, so simple in appearance, has more parts than the human body has limbs: the ring, the stock, the crown, the flukes, the palms, the shank. All this, according to the journalist, is "cast" when a ship arriving at an anchorage is brought up.

This insistence in using the odious word arises from the fact that a particularly benighted landsman must imagine the act of anchoring as a process of throwing something overboard, whereas the anchor ready for its work is already overboard, and is not thrown over, but simply allowed to fall. It hangs from the ship's side at the end of a heavy, projecting timber called the cat-head, in the bight of a short, thick chain whose end link is suddenly released by a blow from a top-maul or the pull of a lever when the order is given. And the order is not "Heave over!" as the paragraphist seems to imagine, but "Let go!"

As a matter of fact, nothing is ever cast in that sense on board ship but the lead, of which a cast is taken to search the depth of water on which she floats. A lashed boat, a spare spar, a cask, or what not secured about the decks, is "cast adrift" when it is untied. Also the ship herself is "cast to port or starboard" when getting under way. She, however, never "casts" her anchor.

To speak with severe technicality, a ship or a fleet is "brought up" — the complementary words unpronounced and unwritten being, of course, "to an anchor." Less technically, but not less correctly, the word "anchored," with its characteristic appearance and resolute sound, ought to be good enough for the newspapers of the greatest maritime country in the world. "The fleet anchored at Spithead": can any one want a better sentence for brevity and seamanlike ring? But the "cast-anchor" trick, with its affectation of being a sea-phrase — for why not write just as well "threw anchor," "flung anchor," or "shied anchor"? — is intolerably odious to a sailor's ear. I remember a coasting pilot of my early acquaintance (he used to read the papers assiduously) who, to define the utmost degree of lubberliness in a landsman, used to say, "He's one of them poor, miserable 'cast-anchor' devils."

II

From first to last the seaman's thoughts are very much concerned with his anchors. It is not so much that the anchor is a symbol of hope as that it is the heaviest object that he has to handle on board his ship at sea in the usual routine of his duties. The beginning and the end of every passage are marked distinctly by work about the ship's anchors. A vessel in the Channel has her anchors always ready, her cables shackled on, and the land almost always in sight. The anchor and the land are indissolubly connected in a sailor's thoughts. But directly she is clear of the narrow seas, heading out into the world with nothing solid to speak of between her and the South Pole, the anchors are got in and the cables disappear from the deck. But the anchors do not disappear. Technically speaking, they are "secured inboard"; and, on the forecastle head, lashed down to ring-bolts with ropes and chains, under the straining sheets of the head sails, they look very idle and as if asleep. Thus bound, but carefully looked after, inert and powerful, those emblems of hope make company for the look-out man in the night watches; and so the days glide by, with a long rest for those characteristically shaped pieces of iron, reposing forward, visible from almost every part of the ship's deck, waiting for their work on the other side of the world somewhere, while the ship carries them

on with a great rush and splutter of foam underneath, and
the sprays of the open sea rust their heavy limbs.

The first approach to the land, as yet invisible to the
crew's eyes, is announced by the brisk order of the chief
mate to the boatswain: "We will get the anchors over this
afternoon" or "first thing to-morrow morning," as the
case may be. For the chief mate is the keeper of the ship's
anchors and the guardian of her cable. There are good
ships and bad ships, comfortable ships and ships where,
from first day to last of the voyage, there is no rest for a
chief mate's body and soul. And ships are what men make
them: this is a pronouncement of sailor wisdom, and, no
doubt, in the main it is true.

However, there are ships where, as an old grizzled mate
once told me, "nothing ever seems to go right!" And,
looking from the poop where we both stood (I had paid
him a neighbourly call in dock), he added: "She's one of
them." He glanced up at my face, which expressed a
proper professional sympathy, and set me right in my
natural surmise: "Oh, no; the old man's right enough.
He never interferes. Anything that's done in a seamanlike
way is good enough for him. And yet, somehow, nothing
ever seems to go right in this ship. I tell you what: she is
naturally unhandy."

The "old man," of course, was his captain, who just
then came on deck in a silk hat and brown overcoat, and,
with a civil nod to us, went ashore. He was certainly not
more than thirty, and the elderly mate, with a murmur to
me of "That's my old man," proceeded to give instances of
the natural unhandiness of the ship in a sort of deprecatory
tone, as if to say, "You mustn't think I bear a grudge
against her for that."

The instances do not matter. The point is that there are
ships where things *do* go wrong; but whatever the ship —
good or bad, lucky or unlucky — it is in the forepart of her

that her chief mate feels most at home. It is emphatically *his* end of the ship, though, of course, he is the executive supervisor of the whole. There are *his* anchors, *his* head-gear, his foremast, his station for manœuvring when the captain is in charge. And there, too, live the men, the ship's hands, whom it is his duty to keep employed, fair weather or foul, for the ship's welfare. It is the chief mate, the only figure of the ship's afterguard, who comes bustling forward at the cry of "All hands on deck!" He is the satrap of that province in the autocratic realm of the ship, and more personally responsible for anything that may happen there.

There, too, on the approach to the land, assisted by the boatswain and the carpenter, he "gets the anchors over" with the men of his own watch, whom he knows better than the others. There he sees the cable ranged, the wind-lass disconnected, the compressors opened; and there, after giving his own last order, "Stand clear of the cable!" he waits attentive, in a silent ship that forges slowly ahead towards her picked-out berth, for the sharp shout from aft, "Let go!" Instantly bending over, he sees the trusty iron fall with a heavy plunge under his eyes, which watch and note whether it has gone clear.

For the anchor "to go clear" means to go clear of its own chain. Your anchor must drop from the bow of your ship with no turn of cable on any of its limbs, else you would be riding to a foul anchor. Unless the pull of the cable is fair on the ring, no anchor can be trusted even on the best of holding ground. In time of stress it is bound to drag, for implements and men must be treated fairly to give you the "virtue" which is in them. The anchor is an emblem of hope, but a foul anchor is worse than the most fallacious of false hopes that ever lured men or nations into a sense of security. And the sense of security, even the most war-ranted, is a bad counsellor. It is the sense which, like that exaggerated feeling of well-being ominous of the coming on of madness, precedes the swift fall of disaster. A seaman labouring under an undue sense of security becomes at once worth hardly half his salt. Therefore, of all my chief officers, the one I trusted most was a man called B——. He had a red moustache, a lean face, also red, and an uneasy eye. He was worth all his salt.

On examining now, after many years, the residue of the feeling which was the outcome of the contact of our personalities, I discover, without much surprise, a certain flavour of dislike. Upon the whole, I think he was one of the most uncomfortable shipmates possible for a young commander. If it is permissible to criticise the absent, I should say he had a little too much of the sense of insecurity which is so invaluable in a seaman. He had an extremely disturbing air of being everlastingly ready (even when seated at table at my right hand before a plate of salt beef) to grapple with some impending calamity. I must hasten to add that he had also the other qualification necessary to make a trustworthy seaman — that of an absolute confidence in himself. What was really wrong with him was that he had these qualities in an unrestful degree. His eternally watchful demeanour, his jerky, nervous talk, even his, as it were, determined silences, seemed to imply — and, I believe, they did imply — that to his mind the ship was never safe in my hands. Such was the man who looked after the anchors of a less than five-hundred-ton barque, my first command, now gone from the face of the earth, but sure of a tenderly remembered existence as long as I live. No anchor could have gone down foul under Mr. B——'s piercing eye. It was good for one to be sure of that when, in an open roadstead, one heard in the cabin the wind pipe up; but still, there were moments when I detested Mr. B—— exceedingly. From the way he used to glare sometimes, I fancy that more than once he paid me back with interest. It so happened that we both loved the little barque very much. And it was just the defect of Mr. B——'s inestimable qualities that he would never persuade himself to believe that the ship was safe in my hands. To begin with, he was more than five years older than myself at a time of life when five years really do count, I being twenty-nine and he thirty-four; then, on our first leaving port (I don't see why I should make a secret of the fact that it was Bangkok), a bit of manœuvring of mine amongst the islands of the Gulf of Siam had given him an unforgettable scare. Ever since then he had nursed in secret a bitter idea of my utter recklessness. But upon the whole, and unless the grip of a man's hand at parting means nothing whatever, I conclude that we did like each other at the end of two years and three months well enough.

The bond between us was the ship; and therein a ship, though she has female attributes and is loved very unreasonably, is different from a woman. That I should have been tremendously smitten with my first command is nothing to wonder at, but I suppose I must admit that Mr. B——'s sentiment was of a higher order. Each of us, of course, was extremely anxious about the good appearance of the beloved object; and, though I was the one to glean compliments ashore, B—— had the more intimate pride of feeling, resembling that of a devoted handmaiden. And that sort of faithful and proud devotion went so far as to make him go about flicking the dust off the varnished teak-wood rail of the little craft with a silk pocket-handkerchief — a present from Mrs. B——, I believe.

That was the effect of his love for the barque. The effect of his admirable lack of the sense of security once went so far as to make him remark to me, "Well, sir, you *are* a lucky man!"

It was said in a tone full of significance, but not exactly offensive, and it was, I suppose, my innate tact that prevented my asking, "What on earth do you mean by that?"

Later on his meaning was illustrated more fully on a dark night in a tight corner during a dead on-shore gale. I had called him up on deck to help me consider our extremely unpleasant situation. There was not much time for deep thinking, and his summing-up was: "It looks pretty bad, whichever we try, but, then, sir, you always do get out of a mess somehow."

III

It is difficult to disconnect the idea of ships' anchors from the idea of the ship's chief mate — the man who sees them go down clear and come up sometimes foul; because not even the most unremitting care can always prevent a ship swinging to winds and tide, from taking an awkward turn of the cable round stock or fluke. Then the business of "getting the anchor" and securing it afterwards is unduly prolonged, and made a weariness to the chief mate. He is the man who watches the growth of the cable — a sailor's phrase which has all the force, precision, and imagery of technical language that, created by simple men with keen eyes for the real aspect of the things they see in their trade, achieves the just expression seizing upon the essential, which is the ambition of the artist in words. Therefore the sailor will never say, "cast anchor," and the shipmaster aft will hail his chief mate on the forecastle in impression-istic phrase: "How does the cable grow?" Because "grow" is the right word for the long drift of a cable emerging aslant under the strain, taut as a bow-string above the water. And it is the voice of the keeper of the ship's anchors that will answer: "Grows right ahead, sir," or "Broad on the bow," or whatever concise and deferential shout will fill the case.

There is no order more noisily given or taken up with

lustier shouts on board a homeward-bound merchant ship than the command, "Man the windlass!" The rush of expectant men out of the forecastle, the snatching of hand-spikes, the tramp of feet, the clink of the pawls, make a stirring accompaniment to a plaintive up-anchor song with a roaring chorus; and this burst of noisy activity from a whole ship's crew seems like a voiceful awakening of the ship herself, till then, in the picturesque phrase of Dutch seaman, "lying asleep upon her iron."

For a ship with her sails furled on her squared yards, and reflected from truck to water-line in the smooth gleaming sheet of a landlocked harbour, seems, indeed, to a seaman's eye the most perfect picture of slumbering repose. The getting of your anchor was a noisy operation on board a merchant ship of yesterday — an inspiring, joyous noise, as if, with the emblem of hope, the ship's company expected to drag up out of the depths, each man all his personal hopes into the reach of a securing hand — the hope of home, the hope of rest, of liberty, of dissipation, of hard pleasure, following the hard endurance of many days between sky and water. And this noisiness, this exultation at the moment of the ship's departure, make a tremendous contrast to the silent moments of her arrival in a foreign road-stead — the silent moments when, stripped of her sails, she forges ahead to her chosen berth, the loose canvas fluttering softly in the gear above the heads of the men standing still upon her decks, the master gazing intently forward from the break of the poop. Gradually she loses her way, hardly moving, with the three figures on her forecastle waiting attentively about the cat-head for the last order of, perhaps, full ninety days at sea: "Let go!"

This is the final word of a ship's ended journey, the closing word of her toil and of her achievement. In a life whose worth is told out in passages from port to port, the splash of the anchor's fall and the thunderous rumbling of the chain are like the closing of a distant period, of which she seems conscious with a slight deep shudder of all her frame. By so much is she nearer to her appointed death, for neither years nor voyages can go on for ever. It is to her like the striking of a clock, and in the pause which follows she seems to take count of the passing time.

This is the last important order; the others are mere routine directions. Once more the master is heard: "Give her forty-five fathom to the water's edge," and then he, too, is done for a time. For days he leaves all the harbour work to his chief mate, the keeper of the ship's anchor and of the ship's routine. For days his voice will not be heard raised about the decks, with that curt, austere accent of the man in charge, till, again, when the hatches are on, and in a silent and expectant ship, he shall speak up from aft in commanding tones: "Man the windlass!"

Progress

Prelude: May, 1919 [1]

FREDERICK LEWIS ALLEN

One morning an author woke and found himself labeled, "Famous Historian." He was slightly bewildered. Frederick Lewis Allen, an essay-writer, had for his own pleasure written a series of essays which formed a panorama of the American scene during the post-war years. Everybody old enough to remember any of the 1920's fell upon *Only Yesterday* with cries of delight and chuckles of remembrance. The book was a best seller for 1932, and two years later was still in strong demand.

The author of *Only Yesterday* is from Boston. He was born in 1890, and was graduated as a member of Harvard's class of 1912. The following year he received a Master of Arts degree from Harvard, and for a while remained at his alma mater to teach. Next he entered the offices of the *Atlantic Monthly* as assistant editor, and in 1916 he became managing editor of the *Century*.

Mr. Allen did publicity work during the War, then in 1919 he returned to Harvard as secretary of the Corporation of Harvard University, serving in this capacity for four years. He is at present in New York, dividing his energies among essay-writing, lecturing, and his duties as associate editor of *Harper's*. During his leisure hours, Mr. Allen enjoys pastel drawing, golf, and Strauss waltzes.

Frederick Lewis Allen has written no fiction, but he has a gift for writing history with a narrative style, which makes his accounts of the very recent past fast and fascinating reading. The essay included here, which is the first chapter of *Only Yesterday*, illustrates the style of Mr. Allen's work, and the pace of the rest of the volume.

↜ ↜

IF TIME were suddenly to turn back to the earliest days of the Post-war Decade, and you were to look about you, what would seem strange to you? Since 1919 the circumstances of American life have been transformed—yes, but exactly how?

---

[1] From *Only Yesterday*, by Frederick Lewis Allen, published by Harper and Brothers. Reprinted by special permission of Harper and Brothers.

Let us refresh our memories by following a moderately well-to-do young couple of Cleveland or Boston or Seattle or Baltimore—it hardly matters which—through the routine of an ordinary day in May, 1919. (I select that particular date, six months after the Armistice of 1918, because by then the United States had largely succeeded in turning from the ways of war to those of peace, yet the profound alterations wrought by the Post-war Decade had hardly begun to take place.) There is no better way of suggesting what the passage of a few years has done to change you and me and the environment in which we live.

§

From the appearance of Mr. Smith as he comes to the breakfast table on this May morning in 1919, you would hardly know that you are not in the nineteen-thirties (though you might, perhaps, be struck by the narrowness of his trousers). The movement of men's fashions is glacial. It is different, however, with Mrs. Smith.

She comes to breakfast in a suit, the skirt of which—rather tight at the ankles—hangs just six inches from the ground. She has read in *Vogue* the alarming news that skirts may become even shorter, and that "not since the days of the Bourbons has the woman of fashion been visible so far above the ankle"; but six inches is still the orthodox clearance. She wears low shoes now, for spring has come; but all last winter she protected her ankles either with spats or with high laced "walking-boots," or with high patent-leather shoes with contrasting buckskin tops. Her stockings are black (or tan, perhaps, if she wears tan shoes); the idea of flesh-colored stockings would appall her. A few minutes ago Mrs. Smith was surrounding herself with an "envelope chemise" and a petticoat; and from the thick ruffles on her undergarments it was apparent that she was not disposed to make herself more boyish in form than ample nature intended.

Mrs. Smith may use powder, but she probably draws the line at paint. Although the use of cosmetics is no longer, in 1919, considered *prima facie* evidence of a scarlet career, and sophisticated young girls have already begun to apply them with some bravado, most well-brought-up women still frown upon rouge. The beauty-parlor industry is in its infancy; there are a dozen hair-dressing parlors for every beauty parlor, and Mrs. Smith has never heard of such dark arts as that of face-lifting. When she puts on her hat to go shopping she will add a veil pinned neatly together behind her head. In the shops she will perhaps buy a bathing-suit for use in the summer; it will consist of an outer tunic of silk or cretonne over a tight knitted undergarment—worn, of course, with long stockings.

Her hair is long, and the idea of a woman ever frequenting a barber shop would never occur to her. If you have forgotten what the general public thought of short hair in those days, listen to the remark of the manager of the Palm Garden in New York when reporters asked him, one night in November, 1918, how he happened to rent his hall for a pro-Bolshevist meeting which had led to a riot. Explaining that a well-dressed woman had come in a fine automobile to make arrangements for the use of the auditorium, he added, "Had we noticed then, as we do now, that she had short hair, we would have refused to rent the hall." In Mrs. Smith's mind, as in that of the manager of the Palm Garden, short-haired women, like long-haired men, are associated with radicalism.

The breakfast to which Mr. and Mrs. Smith sit down may have been arranged with a view to the provision of a sufficient number of calories—they need only to go to Childs' to learn about calories—but in all probability neither of them has ever heard of a vitamin.

As Mr. Smith eats, he opens the morning paper. It is almost certainly not a tabloid, no matter how rudimentary Mr. Smith's journalistic tastes may be: for although Mr. Hearst has already experimented with small-sized picture papers, the first conspicuously successful tabloid is yet to be born. Not until June 26, 1919, will the New York *Daily News* reach the newsstands, beginning a career that will bring its daily circulation in one year to nearly a quarter of a million, in five years to over four-fifths of a million, and in ten years to the amazing total of over one million three hundred thousand.

Strung across the front page of Mr. Smith's paper are head-lines telling of the progress of the American Navy seaplane, the NC-4, on its flight across the Atlantic *via* the Azores. That flight is the most sensational news story of May, 1919. (Alcock and Brown have not yet crossed the ocean in a single hop; they will do it a few weeks hence, eight long years ahead of Lindbergh.) But there is other news, too: of the Peace Conference at Paris, where the Treaty is now in its later stages of preparation; of the successful oversubscription of the Victory Loan ("Sure, we'll finish the job!" the campaign posters have been shouting); of the arrival of another transport with soldiers from overseas; of the threat of a new strike; of a speech by Mayor Ole Hanson of Seattle denouncing the scourge of the times, the I. W. W.; of the prospects for the passage of the Suffrage Amendment, which it is predicted will enable women to take "a finer place in the national life"; and of Henry Ford's libel suit against the Chicago *Tribune*—in the course of which he will call Benedict Arnold a writer, and in reply to the question, "Have there been any revolutions in this country?" will answer, "Yes, in 1812."

If Mr. Smith attends closely to the sporting news, he may find obscure mention of a young pitcher and outfielder for the Boston Red Sox named Ruth. But he will hardly find the Babe's name in the headlines. (In April, 1919, Ruth made one home run; in May, two; but the season was much further advanced before sporting writers began to notice that he was running up a new record for swatting—twenty-nine home runs for the year; the season had closed before the New York Yankees, seeing gold in the hills, bought him for $125,000; and the summer of 1920 had arrived before a man died of excitement when he saw Ruth smash a ball into the bleachers, and it became clear that the mob had found a new idol. In 1919, the veteran Ty Cobb, not Ruth, led the American League in batting.)

The sporting pages inform Mr. Smith that Rickard has selected Toledo as the scene of a forthcoming encounter between the heavyweight champion, Jess Willard, and another future idol of the mob, Jack Dempsey. (They met, you may recall, on the Fourth of July, 1919, and sober citizens were horrified to read that 19,650 people were so depraved as to sit in a broiling sun to watch Dempsey knock out the six-foot-six-inch champion in the third round. How would the sober citizens have felt if they had known that eight years later a Dempsey-Tunney fight would bring in more than five times as much money in gate receipts as this battle of Toledo?) In the sporting pages there may be news of Bobby Jones, the seventeen-year-old Southern golf champion, or of William T. Tilden, Jr., who is winning tennis tournaments here and there, but neither of them is yet a national champion. And even if Jones were to win this year he would hardly become a great popular hero; for although golf is gaining every day in popularity, it has not yet become an inevitable part of the weekly ritual of the American business man. Mr. Smith very likely still scoffs at "grown men who spend their time knocking a little white ball along the ground"; it is quite certain that he has never heard of plus fours; and if he should happen to play golf he had better not show his knickerbockers in the city streets, or small boys will shout to him, "Hey, get some men's pants!"

Did I say that by May, 1919, the War was a thing of the past? There are still reminders of it in Mr. Smith's paper. Not only the news from the Peace Conference, not only the item about Sergeant Alvin York being on his way home; there is still that ugliest reminder of all, the daily casualty list.

Mr. and Mrs. Smith discuss a burning subject, the High Cost of Living. Mr. Smith is hoping for an increase in salary, but meanwhile the family income seems to be dwindling as prices rise. Everything is going up—food, rent, clothing, and taxes. These are the days when people remark that even the man without a dollar is fifty cents better off than he once was, and that if we coined seven-cent pieces for street-car fares, in another year we should have to discontinue them and begin to coin fourteen-cent pieces. Mrs. Smith, confronted with an appeal from Mr. Smith for economy, reminds him that milk has jumped since 1914 from nine to fifteen cents a quart, sirloin steak from twenty-seven to forty-two cents a pound, butter from thirty-two to sixty-one cents a pound, and fresh eggs from thirty-four to sixty-two cents a dozen. No wonder people on fixed salaries are suffering, and colleges are beginning to talk of applying the money-raising methods learned during the Liberty Loan campaigns to the increasing of college endowments. Rents are almost worse than food prices, for that matter; since the Armistice there has been an increasing shortage of houses and apartments, and the profiteering landlord has become an object of popular hate along with the profiteering middleman. Mr. Smith tells his wife that "these profiteers are about as bad as the I. W. W.'s." He could make no stronger statement.

Breakfast over, Mr. Smith gets into his automobile to drive to the office. The car is as likely to be a Lexington, a Maxwell, a Briscoe, or a Templar as to be a Dodge, Buick, Chevrolet, Cadillac, or Hudson, and it surely will not be a Chrysler; Mr. Chrysler has just been elected first vice-president of the General Motors Corporation. Whatever the make of the car, it stands higher than the cars of the nineteen-thirties; the passengers look down upon their surroundings from an imposing altitude. The chances are nine to one that Mr. Smith's automobile is open (only 10.3 per cent of the cars manufactured in 1919 were closed). The vogue of the sedan is just beginning. Closed cars are still associated in the public mind with wealth; the hated profiteer of the newspaper cartoon rides in a limousine.

If Mr. Smith's car is one of the high, hideous, but efficient model T Fords of the day, let us watch him for a minute. He climbs in by the right-hand door (for there is no left-hand door by the front seat), reaches over to the wheel, and sets the spark and throttle levers in a position like that of the hands of a clock at ten minutes to three. Then, unless he has paid extra for a self-starter, he gets out to crank. Seizing the crank in his right hand (carefully, for a friend of his once broke his arm cranking), he slips his left forefinger through a loop of wire that controls the choke. He pulls the loop of wire, he revolves the crank mightily, and as the engine at last roars, he leaps to the trembling runningboard, leans in, and moves the spark and throttle to twenty-five minutes of two. Perhaps he reaches the throttle before the engine falters into silence, but if it is a cold morning perhaps he does not. In that case, back to the crank again and the loop of wire. Mr. Smith wishes Mrs. Smith would come out and sit in the driver's seat and pull that spark lever down before the engine has time to die.

Finally he is at the wheel with the engine roaring as it should. He releases the emergency hand-brake, shoves his left foot against the low-speed pedal, and as the car sweeps loudly out into the street, he releases his left foot, lets the car into high gear, and is off. Now his only care is for that long hill down the street; yesterday he burned his brake on it, and this morning he must remember to brake with the reverse pedal, or the low-speed pedal, or both, or all three in alternation. (Jam your foot down on any of the three pedals and you slow the car.)

Mr. Smith is on the open road—a good deal more open than it will be a decade hence. On his way to work he passes hardly a third as many cars as he will pass in 1929; there are less than seven million passenger cars registered in the United States in 1919, as against over twenty-three million cars only ten years later. He is unlikely to find many concrete roads in his vicinity, and the lack of them is reflected in the speed regulations. A few states like California and New York permit a rate of thirty miles an hour in 1919, but the average limit is twenty (as against thirty-five or forty in 1931). The Illinois rate of 1919 is characteristic of the day; it limits the driver to fifteen miles in residential parts of cities, ten miles in built-up sections, and six miles on curves. The idea of making a hundred-mile trip in two and a half hours—as will constantly be done in the nineteen-thirties by drivers who consider themselves conservative—would seem to Mr. Smith perilous, and with the roads of 1919 to drive on he would be right.

In the course of his day at the office, Mr. Smith discusses business conditions. It appears that things are looking up. There was a period of uncertainty and falling stock prices after the Armistice, as huge government contracts were canceled and plants which had been running overtime on war work began to throw off men by the thousand, but since then conditions have been better. Everybody is talking about the bright prospects for international trade and American shipping. The shipyards are running full tilt. There are too many strikes going on, to be sure; it seems as if the demands of labor for higher and higher wages would never be satisfied, although Mr. Smith admits that in a way you can't blame the men, with prices still mounting week by week. But there is so much business activity that the men being turned out of army camps to look for jobs are being absorbed better than Mr. Smith ever thought they would be. It was back in the winter and early spring that there was so much talk about the ex-service men walking the streets without work; it was then that *Life* ran a cartoon which represented Uncle Sam saying to a soldier, "Nothing is too good for you, my boy! What would you like?" and the soldier answering, "A job." Now the boys seem to be sifting slowly but surely into the ranks of the employed, and the only clouds on the business horizon are strikes and Bolshevism and the dangerous wave of speculation in the stock market.

"Bull Market Taxes Nerves of Brokers," cry the headlines in the financial pages, and they speak of "Long Hours for Clerks." Is there a familiar ring to those phrases? Does it seem natural to you, remembering as you do the Big Bull Market of 1928 and 1929, that the decision to keep the Stock Exchange closed over the 31st of May, 1919, should elicit such newspaper comments as this: "The highly specialized machine which handles the purchase and sales of stocks and bonds in the New York market is fairly well exhausted and needs a rest"? Then listen: in May, 1919, it was a long series of *million-and-a-half-share* days which was causing financiers to worry and the Federal Reserve Board to consider issuing a warning against speculation. During that year a new record of six two-million-share days was set up, and on only 145 days did the trading amount to over a million shares. What would Mr. Smith and his associates think if they were to be told that within eleven years there would occur a sixteen-million-share day; and that they would see the time when three-million-share days would be referred to as "virtual stagnation" or as "listless trading by professionals only, with the general public refusing to become interested"? The price of a seat on the New York Stock Exchange in 1919 ranged between $60,000 and a new high record of $110,000; it would be hard for Mr. Smith to believe that before the end of the decade seats on the Exchange would fetch a half million.

In those days of May, 1919, the record of daily Stock Exchange transactions occupied hardly a newspaper column. The Curb Market record referred to trading on a real curb—to that extraordinary outdoor market in Broad Street, New York, where boys with the telephone receivers clamped to their heads hung out of windows high above the street and grimaced and wigwagged through the din to traders clustered on the pavement below. And if there was anything Mrs. Smith was certain not to have on her mind as she went shopping, it was the price of stocks. Yet the "unprecedented bull market" of 1919 brought fat profits to those who participated in it. Between February 15th and May 14th, Baldwin Locomotive rose from 72 to 93, General Motors from 130 to 191, United States Steel from 90 to $104\frac{1}{2}$, and International Mercantile Marine common (to which traders were attracted on account of the apparently boundless possibilities of shipping) from 23 to $47\frac{5}{8}$.

When Mr. Smith goes out to luncheon, he has to proceed to his club in a roundabout way, for a regiment of soldiers just returned from Europe is on parade and the central thoroughfares of the city are blocked with crowds. It is a great season for parades, this spring of 1919. As the transports from Brest swing up New York Harbor, the men packed solid on the decks are greeted by Mayor Hylan's Committee of Welcome, represented sometimes by the Mayor's spruce young secretary, Grover Whalen, who in later years is to reduce welcoming to a science and raise it to an art. New York City has built in honor of the home-coming troops a huge plaster arch in Fifth Avenue at Madison Square, toward the design of which forty artists are said to have contributed. ("But the result," comments the New York *Tribune*, sadly, "suggests four hundred rather than forty. It holds everything that was ever on an arch anywhere, the lay mind suspects, not forgetting the horses on top of a certain justly celebrated Brandenburg Gate.") Farther up the Avenue, before the Public Library, there is a shrine of pylons and palms called the Court of the Heroic Dead, of whose decorative effect the *Tribune* says, curtly, "Add perils of death." A few blocks to the north an arch of jewels is suspended above the Avenue "like a net of precious stones, between two white pillars surmounted by stars"; on this arch colored searchlights play at night with superb effect.   The Avenue is hung with flags from end to end; and as the Twenty-seventh Division parades under the arches the air is white with confetti and ticker tape, and the sidewalks are jammed with cheering crowds. Nor is New York alone in its enthusiasm for the returning soldiers; every other city has its victory parade, with the city elders on the reviewing stand and flags waving and the bayonets of the troops glistening in the spring sunlight and the bands playing "The Long, Long Trail." Not yet disillusioned, the nation welcomes its heroes—and the heroes only wish the fuss were all over and they could get into civilian clothes and sleep late in the mornings and do what they please, and try to forget.

Mr. and Mrs. Smith have been invited to a tea dance at one of the local hotels, and Mr. Smith hurries from his office to the scene of revelry. If the hotel is up to the latest wrinkles, it has a jazz-band instead of the traditional orchestra for dancing, but not yet does a saxophone player stand out in the foreground and contort from his instrument that piercing music, "endlessly sorrowful yet endlessly unsentimental, with no past, no memory, no future, no hope," which William Bolitho called the *Zeitgeist* of the Post-war Age. The jazz-band plays "I'm Always Chasing Rainbows," the tune which Harry Carroll wrote in wartime after Harrison Fisher persuaded him that Chopin's "Fantasie Impromptu" had the makings of a good ragtime tune. It plays, too, "Smiles" and "Dardanella" and "Hindustan" and "Japanese Sandman" and "I Love You Sunday," and that other song which is to give the

Post-war Decade one of its most persistent and wearisome slang phrases, "I'll Say She Does." There are a good many military uniforms among the fox-trotting dancers. There is one French officer in blue; the days are not past when a foreign uniform adds the zest of wartime romance to any party. In the more dimly lighted palm-room there may be a juvenile petting party or two going on, but of this Mr. and Mrs. Smith are doubtless oblivious. F. Scott Fitzgerald has yet to confront a horrified republic with the Problem of the Younger Generation.

After a few dances, Mr. Smith wanders out to the bar (if this is not a dry state). He finds there a group of men downing Bronxes and Scotch highballs, and discussing with dismay the approach of prohibition. On the 1st of July the so-called Wartime Prohibition Law is to take effect (designed as a war measure, but not signed by the President until after the Armistice), and already the ratification of the Eighteenth Amendment has made it certain that prohibition is to be permanent. Even now, distilling and brewing are forbidden. Liquor is therefore expensive, as the frequenters of midnight cabarets are learning to their cost. Yet here is the bar, still quite legally doing business. Of course there is not a woman within eyeshot of it; drinking by women is unusual in 1919, and drinking at a bar is an exclusively masculine prerogative. Although Mr. and Mrs. Smith's hosts may perhaps serve cocktails before dinner this evening, Mr. and Mrs. Smith have never heard of cocktail parties as a substitute for tea parties.

As Mr. Smith stands with his foot on the brass rail, he listens to the comments on the coming of prohibition. There is some indignant talk about it, but even here the indignation is by no means unanimous. One man, as he tosses off his Bronx, says that he'll miss his liquor for a time, he supposes, but he thinks "his boys will be better off for living in a world where there is no alcohol"; and two or three others agree with him. Prohibition has an overwhelming majority behind it throughout the United States; the Spartan fervor of wartime has not yet cooled. Nor is there anything ironical in the expressed assumption of these men that when the Eighteenth Amendment goes into effect, alcohol will be banished from the land. They look forward vaguely to an endless era of actual drought.

At the dinner party to which Mr. and Mrs. Smith go that evening, some of the younger women may be bold enough to smoke, but they probably puff their cigarettes self-consciously, even defiantly. (The national consumption of cigarettes in 1919, excluding the very large sizes, is less than half of what it will be by 1930.)

After dinner the company may possibly go to the movies to see Charlie Chaplin in "Shoulder Arms" or Douglas Fairbanks in "The Knickerbocker Buckeroo" or Mary Pickford in "Daddy Long Legs" or Theda Bara, or Pearl White, or Griffith's much touted and much wept-at "Broken Blossoms." Or they may play auction bridge (not contract, of course). Mah Jong, which a few years hence will be almost obligatory, is still over the horizon. They may discuss such best sellers of the day as *The Four Horsemen of the Apocalypse*, Tarkington's *The Magnificent Ambersons*, Conrad's *Arrow of Gold*, Brand Whitlock's *Belgium*, and Wells's *The Undying Fire*. (The *Outline of History* is still unwritten.) They may go to the theater: the New York successes of May, 1919, include *Friendly Enemies, Three Faces East*, and *The Better 'Ole*, which have been running ever since wartime and are still going strong, and also *Listen, Lester*, Gillette in *Dear Brutus*, Frances Starr in *Tiger! Tiger!* and —to satisfy a growing taste for bedroom farce—such tidbits as *Up in Mabel's Room*. The Theater Guild is about to launch its first drama, Ervine's *John Ferguson*. The members of the senior class at Princeton have just voted *Lightnin'* their favorite play (after *Macbeth and Hamlet*, for which they cast the votes expected of educated men), and their favorite actresses, in order of preference, are Norma Talmadge, Elsie Ferguson, Marguerite Clark, Constance Talmadge, and Madge Kennedy.

One thing the Smiths certainly will not do this evening. They will not listen to the radio.

For there is no such thing as radio broadcasting. Here and there a mechanically inclined boy has a wireless set, with which, if he knows the Morse code, he may listen to messages from ships at sea and from land stations equipped with sending apparatus. The

radiophone has been so far developed that men flying in an airplane over Manhattan have talked with other men in an office
building below. But the broadcasting of speeches and music—
well, it was tried years ago by DeForest, and "nothing came of
it." Not until the spring of 1920 will Frank Conrad of the Westinghouse Company of East Pittsburgh, who has been sending out
phonograph music and baseball scores from the barn which he
has rigged up as a spare-time research station, find that so many
amateur wireless operators are listening to them that a Pittsburgh
newspaper has had the bright idea of advertising radio equipment "which may be used by those who listen to Dr. Conrad's
programs." And not until this advertisement appears will the
Westinghouse officials decide to open the first broadcasting station
in history in order to stimulate the sale of their supplies.

One more word about Mr. and Mrs. Smith and we may dis-
miss them for the night. Not only have they never heard of radio
broadcasting; they have never heard of Coué, the Dayton Trial,
crossword puzzles, bathing-beauty contests, John J. Raskob,
racketeers, Teapot Dome, Coral Gables, the *American Mercury*,
Sacco and Vanzetti, companionate marriage, brokers' loan sta-
tistics, Michael Arlen, the Wall Street explosion, confession magazines, the Hall-Mills case, Radio stock, speakeasies, Al Capone,
automatic traffic lights, or Charles A. Lindbergh.

The Post-war Decade lies before them.

STUDY HELPS

Note how, in opening the essay, "A Dog in the House," the author begins by discoursing on what makes a house home, implies the presence of children, leads up to the subject of pets, and then dramatically introduces the dog that is to be the topic of the essay. Do you like this opening, or would you have the essay begin with the line, "He seemed all legs, like a cuttle-fish"? Why?

What lines strike you as humorous and tender at the same time?

What passages indicate that the author is a lover of all dogs?

What feelings does he arouse in the reader for the dog he describes?

Explain: "his enormous weeping for infinitesimal punishments."

Do you think this essay should be of interest solely to dog lovers, or should it appeal to everyone?

Explain: "elephantine adolescence."

Explain the allusion: "The Hound of the Baskervilles."

How would you describe Burges Johnson's style of humor?

Write, if you are one of the dog-owning readers, something about your dog. Or if you have never owned a dog, tell whether you wish you might have one, and why.

"Gulliver the Great" is a short story about a dog, written by Walter Dyer. Do you know any other story about a Dane, true or fiction? If so, give an oral report of it.

. . .

In what field of literature is A. A. Milne's best work?

What do you think of his style?

Has he captured the mood of a boy at the end of a holiday, or have the "hundred years" which he says have elapsed caused him to view the situation in a false light?

He exaggerates for effect. Too much so, do you think? Find examples of good effect achieved through slight exaggeration.

What is gained by use of the editorial "we"?

Is he convincing in describing the happiest half-hours of his life?

What are some outstanding differences between Robert Benchley's style of humor and Burges Johnson's?

Try to describe the nature of the humor in each essay.

Do you think Mr. Benchley is original, or do you know other writers who rely on similar effects to provoke laughs?

At what point in this essay does the humor become apparent, forgetting the fact that you invariably associate Robert Benchley's name with humorous writing?

What impressions of the author do you get from reading this piece? Do the biographical notes sustain this impression?

What lines cause a faint smile? Which ones produce a hearty laugh? Do you find some that are really clever?

Mr. Benchley's popularity has been attributed to the fact that he always makes himself the butt of his own jokes, whereas some jokesters turn the laugh on the reader. Is this statement applicable to the essay you have just read? Do you think it might explain successful humor?

Read more of Robert Benchley in *Of All Things*, *The Early Worm*, or *The Treasurer's Report*, and analyze further the effect of this contention.

. . .

What is the mood of the essay "Real People"?

How in the opening lines are you made aware of it?

How would you describe Mr. Strunsky's style of humor?

Does the essay give you any idea as to the kind of man the author is? The agent?

Compare Mr. Strunsky's writing with Burges Johnson's and Robert Benchley's. In what ways does it differ from each of these?

What do you think Mr. Strunsky's attitude is toward Emmeline's choice of apartments?

How much do you believe he has exaggerated the faults of the apartment?

Is this a well-planned essay?

WIT VERSUS HUMOR

Charles Brooks and Stephen Leacock, authors of widely divergent style, both compare wit with humor. Do you find any similarity in their ideas?

What differences in style are most evident? Which author has the most facile style?

Notice Brooks's easy-flowing, unusual figures of speech, and

Leacock's turning of an unexpected phrase to obtain a humorous effect. Find several examples of each of these.

Can you draw a definite comparison between wit and humor?

Considering his essay, what kind of personality do you believe Mr. Brooks to have?

Is his a humorous or a serious essay?

Do you think his generalities in summing up the witty and the humorous man are always accurate?

Explain: "Wit is as sharp as lightning, whereas humor is diffuse like sunlight."

What is his explanation of the fact that the witticisms of the past are dull reading today?

Does this essay show careful planning and logical coördination, or is it rambling? Give examples to support your answer.

Do you think that Stephen Leacock exaggerates for effect? If so, is it overdone?

Leacock has a knack of hitting upon the weaknesses and absurd vanities of human nature. Would you call his writing witty or humorous? What to him is the essence of good humor?

At what similar conclusions do Brooks and Leacock arrive in closing their essays?

THE COLLEGE QUESTION

Probably no high-school senior has reached that grade without having formed some plan, vague or definite, for the future. This article by Dean McConn should be helpful to every senior-high-school student, for it provides specific standards by which each student may honestly appraise himself and his aptitudes and abilities. It is natural to see ourselves as we should like to be, rather than as we are.

If you are planning to go to college, have you thought of your ability to do the work there, or has the main object seemed to be the thrill of going away to school, or of social success? In other words, have you been concerning yourself with the main purpose of a college education?

You can probably think of several students who, within the last few years, graduated from your school well down in the second half of their class. According to Dean McConn, such students faced grave danger of failure in college. Have your friends succeeded? What, in that case, is your answer to the writer's contention?

NATIONAL COUNCIL OF TEACHERS OF ENGLISH [1]

Tentative (Experimental) Rating-Scale for Judging Photoplays and Measuring Appreciation—Grades 9 and 10

Name of Pupil _____ Age _____ Sex _____ Grade _____ School _____ City _____

Name of Picture _____ Producer _____ Author _____ Director _____ Star _____

				Score	Wgt.	Weighted Score
Fundamental Idea	Unimportant −2 (very) −1 (rather)	Not Clear 0	Important +1 (rather) +2 (very)		10	
Story Structure	Illogical −2 (very) −1 (rather)	Trite 0	Logical +1 (rather) +2 (very)		20	
Characters	Artificial −2 (very) −1 (rather)	Colorless 0	Life-like +1 (rather) +2 (very)		15	
Setting and Photography	Inappropriate or Crude −2 (very) −1 (rather)	Acceptable 0	Beautiful or Appropriate +1 (rather) +2 (very)		5	
Dialogue	Dull −2 (very) −1 (rather)	Ordinary 0	Bright +1 (rather) +2 (very)		5	
Value to Society	Destructive −2 (very) −1 (rather)	Doubtful 0	Constructive +1 (rather) +2 (very)		10	
Acting	False or Exaggerated −2 (very) −1 (rather)	Commonplace 0	Sincere or Natural +1 (rather) +2 (very)		10	
Speech	Defective −2 (very) −1 (rather)	Not Noticeable 0	Effective +1 (rather) +2 (very)		5	
Direction	Uninspired −2 (very) −1 (rather)	Mediocre 0	Imaginative +1 (rather) +2 (very)		10	
Enjoyment	Uninteresting −2 (very) −1 (rather)	Neutral 0	Interesting +1 (rather) +2 (very)		10	

Total Score ....
Percentage Score ....

Note: The score which the pupil assigns to each item, multiplied by the weight, gives the weighted score. Highest possible score is 200. To obtain percentage score, divide total score by 2.

[1] Reprinted by permission of Mr. William Lewin, Chairman of the Committee on Photoplay Appreciation, 1934 — National Council of English Teachers.

NATIONAL COUNCIL OF TEACHERS OF ENGLISH [1]

TENTATIVE RATING-SCALE FOR JUDGING PHOTOPLAYS AND MEASURING APPRECIATION—GRADES 11 AND 12

Name of Pupil .... Age .... Sex .... Grade .... School .... Director .... City

Name of Picture .... Producer .... Author .... Star

	−1	0	+1	+2	+3	Score	Wgt.	Weighted Score
BASIC THEME	Lacking	Of Little or No Importance	Timely, Significant	Vitally Important	Momentous, Epical		10	
STORY COMPOSITION	Incoherent	Possible, but Not Plausible	Rather Logical	Highly Probable	Flawless in Continuity		20	
CHARACTERIZATIONS	Overdrawn, Unnatural	Rather Stereotyped	Likable	Touching	Genuine		15	
DIALOGUE	Trite	Colorless	Rather Witty	Clever	Brilliant		5	
VOICE OF STAR	Annoying, Defective	Rather Uncultured	Not Very Noticeable	Effective	Remarkably Versatile		5	
ACTING OF STAR	Overdone	Obviously Artificial	Casual	Subtle, Charming	Sincere, Life-like		10	
DIRECTION	Weak, Dull	Irregular	Smooth	Swift, Convincing	Strikingly Imaginative		10	
PICTORIAL COMPOSITION	Ugly	Ordinary	Appropriate	Unusual in Photography	Consistently Beautiful		5	
SOCIAL VALUE	Destructive	Harmless	Wholesome	Commendable	Inspiring to High Ideals		10	
ENJOYMENT	Disgusting, Boring	Little or No Interest	Entertaining	Thrilling	Absorbing		10	

TOTAL SCORE ....
PERCENTAGE SCORE ....

Note: The score which the pupil assigns to each item, multiplied by the weight, gives the weighted score. Highest possible total score is 300. To obtain percentage score, divide total score by 3.

[1] Reprinted by permission of Mr. William Lewin, Chairman of the Committee on Photoplay Appreciation, 1934 — National Council of English Teachers.

Suppose two students in the lower half of their high-school class go to the same college. One fails and the other makes good. Is that an argument for or against recommending college to poor students?

What does Dr. McConn consider the three major requirements to determine college material? After considering them carefully, which one in itself seems most desirable?

There are always some high-school graduates who qualify in all three of these criteria, but have not the means to go to college. Does your school have any desirable scholarships for such students? Discuss a plan for further scholarship aid.

What are some arguments for and against making scholarships a part of the local school budget?

.   .   .

Does Heywood Broun's essay give you anything new to think about?

Is he a person qualified to discuss sports?

Do you agree with his attitude or feel inclined to dispute his arguments?

Have you ever considered that there might be an argument against scholastic football?

What are Mr. Broun's objections to amateur football? Can you think of an argument to refute or to sustain any of his objections?

What effect is achieved by the opening words of this essay?

Do you think the episode of the dropped punt is as serious as the writer contends?

Explain the paradoxical statement that a boy of nineteen is hurt by losing a game no less than he is hurt by winning.

Do you think the description of a coach's appeal to the emotions of the players is exaggerated? If not, is it justifiable?

What is Heywood Broun's attitude toward amateur and professional athletics?

Do you think the qualities he admires in Babe Ruth are true generally of professional athletes?

The paragraph describing the cheering at a football game and the applause at a baseball game is a typically Broun paragraph. Can you refute any of his statements? What is the purpose of the courtesy cheer? Is it fair of Broun to ridicule this custom?

Has this essay changed your opinion in the slightest regarding the merits of scholastic football?

Read other articles by Heywood Broun. Then decide in what ways this essay is typical of his style and treatment.

PERSONAL REACTIONS

What is the author's definition of "hard boiled"? Do you like it? Could you improve on the definition?

Do you think it pays to be hard boiled? Can you cite some example to support your argument?

In general, does mankind admire a person who is hard boiled?

Is the distinction between a hard-boiled brain and a hard-boiled heart well made?

Mr. Terhune has strong feelings on the subject of tipping. What is your feeling on the matter? Do you think the practice should be abolished?

What do you think of the attitude of a man like Smithers? Would he do better to be openly generous?

Does a very wealthy man need to build defenses to protect himself?

Has Mr. Terhune thrown practical light on any social problems?

READING AND WRITING

Notice how Professor MacMechan introduces his delightful essay on a topic which could well be classed as unpromising and certainly as uninspiring. Opening his discussion with the Latin version of the first line of Psalm 103, "I have cried out from the deep," the author chooses to capitalize upon rather than to excuse the complete incongruity of the scenic background and the lowly task which he has chosen for his exposition.

Keeping the important details of the author's life in mind, and in the light of the names included in the first paragraph, what Province of the Dominion forms the probable setting for this essay?

After having read this essay, check the degree of success which the author has attained in his exposition by listing as many of the important details to be borne in mind while searching for and digging clams that you can recall without further reference to the essay itself.

. .

What is your opinion of Dorothy Canfield's assertion that no one ever learns easily how to write well?

In what way is self-discipline necessary in the task of writing?

Please note the statement, "cutting out the whiches." Why is that a phrase which all of us would do well to remember permanently?

Explain: inertia, repugnance, inhibition, spasm.

Notice the clarity of thought and expression evident in this theme. Pick out the topic sentences in paragraphs two, three, and four, and describe how the author is building up her theme. Point out the transitory sentences and other evidences of her manner of securing a unified and coherent finished product.

IN FOREIGN PLACES

Cuyp: The name of a Dutch family which produced two genera- tions of painters. The best-known member was Albert Cuyp (1620-1691), probably one of van Goyen's pupils. Albert Cuyp specialized in painting Dutch pastoral scenes.

Riemann: Georg Friedrich Bernhard Riemann (1826-1866), a well-known German mathematician.

Polder: An area of reclaimed land in Holland lying below the level of the sea.

Caves of Altamira: Prehistoric caves in Spain.

Lake Dwellings of Glastonbury: A reference to the prehistoric lake-village which has been discovered in the meadowland near Glastonbury, England.

paralogism: false reasoning, or bad logic.

.   .   .

In this essay the author draws a sharp contrast between two different "views" of Holland. What are these different "views"? Which view-point appeals most to the author?

Are you able to tell from which point of view each of the descriptive paragraphs is taken?

How does the very last sentence sum up the whole theme of the essay? In the light of recent events, could any author today give a description of Holland from the same point of view which Huxley assumes at the beginning of this essay?

Write an essay using the same treatment as Aldous Huxley by describing your subject from two or more points of view. Choose for your composition some country or place which you have visited. You might contrast the relatively peaceful scene from the top of a sky-scraper with the return to reality which you meet in the bustle of traffic as you come out the main entrance. Perhaps you have been through the Canadian Rockies, and can contrast the life and scenery you have found in the valleys with its appearance from a great height or distance. It may be that a parallel scene which you have noticed near your own home will occur to you. In any event, you should endeavour to make the contrast between the two view-points as sharp as possible, first, by choosing a suitable subject for your essay, and second, by balancing different descriptions of corresponding portions of the scenery against each other. Huxley has used points of view which differ from each other only mentally. It is not as difficult to describe a scene from two points of view which differ physically, but care should be taken to *maintain* the *contrast* throughout the essay rather than to let it become simply a double description.

. . .

"Within gunreach in front of me trudged my little Akawai Indian hunter." How do you think a less facile writer than Beebe might have opened this essay?

What is the humour of calling the Indian "Nupee"?

Beebe attempts to make his reader see and feel the mystery of that moonlight-flooded scene. Does he succeed?

The unexplained "strange midnight revel" of the goatsuckers lends what atmosphere to the vivid picture? How is a touch of amusement introduced?

Explain: "bleached, ashamed trunks."

Alone at night in the jungle, how does Mr. Beebe feel as a member of the all-powerful race of man?

Do not miss this line: "It is the most weirdly beautiful of all places outside the world."

Are you able to imagine the feeling he describes of seeming to exist only in the senses of sight and smell and hearing?

What gives reality to the Indian superstitions about the tree frog?

Notice the skill of Mr. Beebe's writing—how he introduces the light touch of amusement, without ever letting it impair the atmosphere of awe and mystery which he creates so convincingly. Find one or two examples of this.

Why is Mr. Beebe quite certain that his unreasoning turn of thoughts to the "poor-me-one" was not a coincidence?

Notice that a scientist's interest is large enough to encompass every detail of sight, sound, and smell; that on a hunt for the rare armadillo he can still pause to capture an amusing beetle, to notice the scent of orchids, and to note the voices of frogs and crickets. Never once does a note of fear or personal danger creep into his mood. Confronted by a giant serpent, he contemplates its existence: "Is there any stranger life in the world?"

Why does the monkey ladder's fall seem to the scientist the most significant event of the night's happenings?

Why does he not want to wait for the dawn?

"Alone with your thoughts at night." Describe the situation and your reaction.

CONCERNING WOMEN

What do you think of Mrs. Banning's list of things expected of a seventeen-year-old girl? Would you cross anything off that list, or add to it?

Has this mother considered every possibility in trying to prepare her girl for the future?

Check your own abilities against Mrs. Banning's list of what a young girl should know. Do you think more than this is expected of a boy?

Could any bright girl equip herself to meet the requirements enumerated, regardless of her financial status?

What is your personal reaction to this essay?

OF SHIPS AND TRAVEL

How, in his first paragraph which consists of only two sentences, does Christopher Morley at once introduce the general background, the immediate locale, and the main "character" of his essay?

What is the mood of his second paragraph? How and where is it changed with one swift stroke?

What is your mental picture of Buck McNeil?

The harbour of any big city is a place of seething activity. The Battery in New York is one of the most interesting places in the city. If you are familiar with this spot, describe your impressions of it, or of some shipping point which you do know.

How many members of the Three Hours for Lunch Club accompanied Mr. Morley on this afternoon on a tugboat?

What ideas do you form about this Club? Mr. Morley tells us little about it, yet we may get some idea of its members, its purpose, and its activities.

Would you have thought, before reading this essay, that a tugboat could be an interesting place on which to spend an afternoon?

What are some of the duties of a tugboat captain?

Note some of Christopher Morley's graphic, brief descriptions, as: the *Alaskan* "came striding up the Narrows." Find other examples.

What are some of the harbour sights and activities which impress this author?

Is Mr. Morley a lover of the sea? What does he mean by "prima donnas"?

Tugboats remind Morley of what animal? Do you think his comparison a good one? How many places do you find in which he uses this figure of speech?

"*Aquitania* loomed up in the haze." Is this abrupt sentence an effective description of the arrival of the great steamship?

What are the writer's feelings about her?

What are his emotions during the docking of the ocean liner?

In what important ways does this essay differ from a short story? Do you think it might have been written in short story form?

What mood prevails when the afternoon on the *Alice M. Moran* is ended?

Has Christopher Morley succeeded in getting his emotions into words?

Write a description of a tugboat, trying for brevity and colour.

.   .   .

Why does the author refer to ships' anchors as "Emblems of Hope"?

Sum up the feelings which must have existed between the chief officer, B——, and the author. Was there any real spirit of animosity between them? From the author's description of their relationship, would you gather that they each respected the other's ability?

Notice how the author sees romance attached to the common-place tasks and objects of sea life. Outline instances in this essay in which he adds colour and glamour to everyday scenes and routine events.

PROGRESS

How do you imagine a high-school boy or girl would have looked in 1919?

What points of similarity do you find between the Smiths' conversation, thoughts, and routine, and those of an ordinary family today?

What differences are the most striking; the most amusing?

We are inclined while we are young to think the things we are doing and saying at the moment are more important and interesting than anything that has ever been said or done before. Does this picture of people in 1919 affect our sense of superiority in any way?

Of the "news" appearing in the papers on that May morning in 1919, what subjects and what personalities continue to be interesting today?

What is your opinion of tabloid newspapers, and how do you account for their astonishing growth?

What were the "I. W. W.'s"?

What is the Brandenburg Gate, and what does the criticism of the New York *Tribune* mean?

Explain: "Not yet disillusioned, the nation welcomes its heroes."

Slang has been termed "an idiom on trial." As an experiment in spoken English, you might be interested in exhuming some of the slang in use in 1919. See whether any of it has survived the "trial," and become accepted as an idiom; or whether it is obsolete. Contrasted with slang phrases now in use, how does it sound? How many popular slang expressions of today have a chance of surviving?

Of the songs, plays, movie stars, and authors popular in 1919, how many are still remembered?

Does the author feel that it is an intellectual pose for the Princeton seniors to vote *Macbeth* and *Hamlet* their favourite plays?

As a matter of fact, do you think such a vote was a "pose"?

"The Post-war Decade lies before them." Does this closing paragraph arouse your curiosity, and make you wish to read more of the swift-moving account of the past decade?